daughter of the Father heals the rupture between us and God.' For every woman willing to embrace her journey, this book is an indispensable guide."

— Denise Easter-Kramer
Easter's Catholic Books and Gifts,
Sacramento, CA

"This work of Katrina Zeno is a major contribution to the understanding of womanhood in the modern world. It is very practical, beautiful, and a complement to the work now being done by myself and others on masculine Catholic identity. Katrina's warmth and femininity radiates throughout her book. I recommend that women gather in small groups to slowly study and discuss this wonderful work."

— Philip J. Mango, Ph.D.
President, St. Michael's Institute for the
Psychological Sciences

"In a simple yet powerful style, Katrina presents deep insights into the dignity and identity of women. Her explanation of John Paul II's theology of the body and his concept of the 'genius of women' left me reflecting on my own journey long after I put the book down."

— Vicki Crispo
Missionaries of the Gospel of Life

Discovering the
feminine
genius

Every Woman's Journey

By Katrina J. Zeno

auline
BOOKS & MEDIA
Boston

Library Library of Congress Cataloging-in-Publication Data

Zeno, Katrina J.
  Discovering the feminine genius : every woman's journey / Katrina Zeno.
    p. cm.
  ISBN 0-8198-1884-4 (pbk.)
  1. Catholic women—Religious life. I. Title.
  BX2353.Z42 2010
  248.8'43—dc22

2009042460

The Scripture quotations contained herein are from the *New Revised Standard Version Bible: Catholic Edition*, copyright © 1989, 1993, Division of Christian Education of the National Council of the Churches of Christ in the United States of America. Used by permission. All rights reserved.

Excerpts from the English translation of the *Catechism of the Catholic Church* for use in the United States of America, copyright © 1994, United States Catholic Conference, Inc. — Libreria Editrice Vaticana. Used with permission.

Quotations from Pope John Paul II used with the permission of the Libreria Editrice Vaticana, 00120, Città del Vaticana.

Excerpt taken from Hans Urs von Balthasar, *You Crown the Year with Your Goodness: Sermons Throughout the Liturgical Year* (San Francisco: Ignatius Press, 1989). Used with permission.

Many manufacturers and sellers distinguish their products through the use of trademarks. Any trademark designations that appear in this book are used in good faith but are not authorized by, associated with, or sponsored by the trademark owners.

Cover design by Rosanna Usselmann

Cover photo by felinda / istockphoto.com

"P" and PAULINE are registered trademarks of the Daughters of St. Paul.

Published by Pauline Books & Media, 50 Saint Paul's Avenue, Boston, MA 02130-3491

Printed in the U.S.A.

www.pauline.org

Pauline Books & Media is the publishing house of the Daughters of St. Paul, an international congregation of women religious serving the Church with the communications media.

1 2 3 4 5 6 7 8   9 14 13 12 11 10

In memory of Pope John Paul II,
my spiritual father,
who showed the world
how to make
a sincere gift of self.

Contents

Introduction

ON JUNE 16, 1992, I met the pope! It was two days before my son's fifth birthday, and we had requested to attend John Paul II's private morning Mass in Rome as a special birthday blessing.

Our request was granted, and, after Mass, we were ushered into a large audience hall outside his private chapel. As John Paul II shuffled to greet each collection of visitors, he was visibly in pain. However, his face lit up whenever a child or baby was in the group.

Our turn quickly arrived, and John Paul II handed each of us a papal Rosary. In return, my son handed him a small book, *The Titles of Mary*. Delighted, the Holy Father bent down, embraced my son, and kissed him. Then he placed his hand on my forehead and blessed me.

It was a blessing I will never forget. The vicar of Christ imparted a portion of his spirit to me. Next to the birth of my son, it was the most beautiful moment of my life.

In my spirit, I sensed I received new graces for motherhood. These graces were indeed for motherhood, but not

biological motherhood. They were for spiritual motherhood.

At the time, I didn't even know such a thing existed—
that I, as a single mother and laywoman, could be a spiritual
mother. I was still navigating the turbulent waters of an
annulled marriage. But God was way ahead of me. He was
already charting a new course and infusing my being with the
grace I would need. He was also introducing me to my spiritual father, John Paul II, who would guide me through the
process of discovering the beauty of the feminine genius
along with the meaning and purpose of the body.

The meaning and purpose of the body? Who ever thinks
of such a thing! As busy women, we rarely take time out to
focus on the intricacies of our (very complicated!) spiritual
journeys, much less why God created us with *this* particular
body. More often, we get along on minimal or maintenance
rations — giving ourselves just enough emotional and spiritual food to get through each day. Yet, deep down, we feel a
deeper yearning. We want to know there's more to life than
conquering ten loads of laundry, correcting homework, or
searching for "the one" on an Internet dating site. Every once
in a while the insistent cry of our heart escapes and we dare
to ask: "Who am I?"

If you've ever asked yourself this question, you are not
alone! Mothers who have packed their last child off to college,
widows who have felt dismissed from life, and single professional women hemmed in by the dull routine of everyday life
have all breached this same question. Now through the
insights of Pope John Paul II and his theology of the body, we

as women can tackle this question with fresh energy and vigor. We can lift the curtain on the feminine genius and discover its meaning for every woman's journey and definitively answer the question: "Who am I?"

CHAPTER 1

First a Daughter, Then a Bride

LIFE WAS SUPPOSED TO BE oh, so simple: I'd grow up, get married, have a family, enjoy my grandchildren, sit in the sun during retirement, and die at a happy old age. But that's not what happened.

Somewhere along the line, the Author forgot the story line. It changed. I changed. My whole world changed. I had to search for a new identity, a new understanding of God, and a new mission. Instead of getting the life I signed up for, I had to discover the one God designed for me from all eternity.

My life had all the makings of *Fortune 500* success. I was born and raised in San Diego, California, when it was a sleepy big city. Located one mile from the beach, our house was perched on a mountain that connected the middle-class suburb of Pacific Beach to the ritzy suburb of La Jolla. I could walk to public grade school and then later bike to my high school on Mission Bay.

As a teenager, I thought nothing of taking the bus by myself to downtown San Diego for gymnastics, or of play-

ing hide-and-seek with my friends in the world-famous San
Diego Zoo. Life was safe, secure, and comfortable.

Ditto for home. As the fifth of six children in a wonderful
Catholic family, I thought everyone grew up with their father
emptying the dishwasher, taking the family camping for vaca-
tion, having meals together, and playing "spoons" until mid-
night on New Year's Eve.

My Catholic upbringing was especially rich. My mother was
ahead of her time. Or, I should say, Mary Reed Newland,[1]
whom my mother read and imitated, was ahead of her time.

There was no need for Santa Claus in our home. We fes-
tively celebrated Saint Nick and his feast day on December 6.
Lent meant getting a purple bean for each sacrifice we made
and praying the Stations of the Cross with fourteen candles.

Holy Thursday found us gathered around the Passover
table, where the menu included bitter herbs (from the dande-
lions in our front lawn) and red bricks made from gelatin. We
spent Good Friday in quiet from noon until 3:00 P.M., with the
phone off the hook and a "do not disturb" sign on the front
door. My family celebrated baptismal days, feast days, Advent,
and Pentecost in creative, tangible ways.

Getting to Know Him

Even with this rich upbringing, I lacked one thing. I knew
a lot about Jesus, but I didn't know Jesus personally. It would
be as if I told you about my good friend, Maureen. She has red
hair and freckles, played the trombone in high school, and is
easygoing. However, you wouldn't know her personally until
I actually introduced you to her face to face. It was the same

with Jesus. I knew a lot about him, but I didn't know him personally.

All that changed when I was sixteen. While most of my peers were rejecting religion, I attended a Youth Encounter Retreat weekend. I noticed that the people there had something I didn't have. I didn't know what it was, but I wanted to find out. As the retreat progressed, I heard for the first time that I could give my life to Jesus and know him personally as a close friend.

I took the plunge. On Sunday of the retreat, I asked my small group to pray for me to give my life to Jesus. As they prayed, I cried. As they continued to pray, I continued to cry. When they stopped praying, I was still crying. I felt as if Mount Olympus had been lifted from my shoulders even though I didn't know why I was crying.

Of course, I realize now that God was answering my prayer. He was helping me release my life to him, with all its pent-up hurts and anxieties. Jesus was no longer someone "out there." He was now close and personal. I'd met God face to face, or more accurately, heart to heart.

A new life began for me that day, although I didn't experience a dramatic external change. I was a straight-A student, I never smoked or drank, and I obeyed my parents. However, an interior change began to take place. God had taken the central place in my life. Jesus was becoming my best friend, and I started reading the Bible to get to know God better.

In the brashness of my late teens I can remember thinking I was never going to go through crisis. I knew my identity was in God and that was that. It would carry me through to my grave.

I was wrong.

Over the past twenty-five years, and especially the past fifteen, I have asked myself many, many times: "Who am I?" It's amazing how many times in life we revisit this question. It's like a pesky fly that won't go away. You bat at it, and it goes away for a while, but it returns again and again. Finally, out of desperation, you get a fly swatter and smack, victory at last! But it's only for a little while, until you hear bzzz, bzzz … and the cycle starts all over again.

How do we deal with this pesky fly that won't leave us alone? Is it possible to answer the question "Who am I?" once and for all?

I thought I had the answer down pat: At sixteen, I had given my life to Christ and made him the focus of my identity. At eighteen, I graduated as valedictorian of my high school with a 4.0 GPA. At nineteen, I married my high school sweetheart, and at twenty-one, I left San Diego to study theology at Franciscan University of Steubenville in Ohio. (Yes, you read it right. I left San Diego for *Ohio*.)

In Ohio, we had a couple of rough transition years, but we managed. We became part of a dynamic Catholic community of families. I graduated third in my college class and received the senior theology award. My husband opened his own business. I worked for a pro-life organization for a year, and then our wonderful son, Michael, was born.

I had the life I signed up for—a good husband, a healthy son, Christian fellowship, intellectual stimulation, supportive relationships, and a home in a nice neighborhood. My life was like a seamless garment. Everything was neatly connected: my social life, spiritual life, part-time work, and intellectual life all revolved around the same Catholic community.

Then the garment began to unravel. For many years my husband had struggled with his personal identity. God intervened at certain crisis points and the issue would go underground for a while, but it would always pop up again. I'd run out of strategies for dealing with this. We'd moved, we'd joined a Catholic community, and we'd started our family, but the issue kept resurfacing.

When our son, Michael, was almost three, my husband and I agreed on a temporary separation, intending to later get back together after working through the conflicts. Over the next year, I went through one of the darkest periods in my life. So much pain saturated my mind that I couldn't think of praying in a conversational way. I turned to rote prayers to give me words to say. I beseeched the heavens for help and discovered Mary as my mother and the saints as my friends.

During this time, my friends often urged me to call them when I was feeling down. I quickly realized this was impossible. I couldn't pick up the phone and say, "Hi, this is Katrina. I just called to tell you I'm feeling numb and depressed and I'm not even sure I'm going to make it."

I couldn't do it. I needed them to call me. So I asked five women in my faith sharing group to each take one day of the week and call me. With their help, I made it through the worst month of my life and started inching toward the top of the pit.

Then God broke through my darkness.

One night at a women's prayer meeting, I felt suddenly bathed in a shaft of light. I stood there soaking in the light, because up to that point I hadn't realized how dark the darkness had been.

In that moment, God showed me the value of contrast.

Just as parents teach their children right/left, up/down, in/out, stop/go, so, too, the Lord teaches us through contrast. He teaches us through light and darkness, fullness and aridity, joy and sorrow, intimacy and abandonment. I was so thankful the light had come and pierced my darkness, even though it didn't remove all the pain.

What was the source of my pain? It was the pain of a crushed identity. My whole adult life I had lived and breathed in the atmosphere of marriage as a sacrament, as a reflection of Christ's unbreakable bond of love for the Church. Because of my role as a youth leader and then a parish catechist, my friends and family all knew that I believed in marriage as a permanent commitment. But now, with my marriage failing, I was no longer a reflection of Christ's permanent love for the Church. I felt as if someone had taken my identity, placed it on a table and smashed it into a million pieces. The seamless garment wasn't just unraveling; it was being ripped in two.

First a Daughter, Then a Bride!

But the Lord taught me something that year on my thirtieth birthday that completely changed my life. In prayer, he told me I was first a daughter, then a bride.

First a daughter, then a bride! Somewhere along the way in trying to figure out my identity as a woman, I'd forgotten the most fundamental truth of my life: before being a wife, mother, friend, teacher, or student, I was first a daughter of God. In his mercy, God ripped out the faulty foundation of straw and hay that he knew wouldn't last and was laying a new one of gold and precious stones.

I even stumbled on a Scripture that aptly described my situation:

> For your Maker is your husband,
> the LORD of hosts is his name;
> the Holy One of Israel is your Redeemer,
> the God of the whole earth he is called.
> For the Lord has called you
> like a wife forsaken and grieved in spirit,
> like the wife of a man's youth when she is cast off,
> says your God.
> For a brief moment I abandoned you,
> but with great compassion I will gather you.
> In overflowing wrath for a moment
> I hid my face from you,
> but with everlasting love I will have compassion on you,
> says the Lord, your Redeemer. (Is 54:5–8)

Since my thirtieth birthday I have never been the same. Certainly, I've had to revisit many issues I thought were closed: Should I marry? Should I stay single? Should I work? How much should I work? Should I stay in Steubenville? Should I move back to San Diego? But the one question I've never had to ask myself again is "Who am I in the eyes of God?" Ever since that life-changing day, my feminine identity has been securely rooted in the truth that I am first a daughter, then a bride.

For every woman, this is the starting point of the journey: to know she is a daughter of God before anything else. This is the rock-solid foundation that no amount of rain, wind, disaster, or pain can destroy.

Why is this so important? Because knowing the Father's love is the heart of the Gospel message. Jesus' mission encompassed many dimensions, including revealing God as "Abba," "Father." When the disciples asked Jesus to teach them to pray, he began: "Abba, who art in heaven...." In Romans 8:15, Saint Paul pens the perfect message to announce the Fatherhood of God: "You did not receive a spirit of slavery leading you back into fear, but a spirit of adoption through which we cry out, '*Abba!*' (that is 'Father')." That message belongs on every billboard on every road to constantly remind us of this indelible truth.

Dismissing Fatherhood

The tragedy of modern culture is its attempt to remove the billboard, to wipe out the Fatherhood of God. Nothing could be more harmful to the journey, to discovering our identity as women. If God isn't our Father, then we aren't his daughters. And if we aren't his daughters, then we are orphans. We're alone and destitute, with no one to help us.

A friend of mine once described her fear of being an orphan in this way: She saw herself as a little girl running down the sidewalk, when suddenly she fell flat on her face. Her automatic response was to stuff away the pain, scrape herself off the sidewalk, and keep going.

One day, in prayer, she felt the Lord telling her to remain on the sidewalk, and to wait face down. Fear gripped her being! She was scared no one would come to help her. She was afraid God would leave her there as an orphan.

God the Father did come to help, and it was one of the biggest breakthroughs in her spiritual life. She finally realized she didn't have to do it on her own. She experienced God as Father and herself as a beloved daughter.

This attack on the Fatherhood of God didn't originate with modern culture. It was Satan's strategy from the beginning. Ever since Adam and Eve, Satan has been trying to convince us we're orphans, that we don't have a loving Father, and we'll be left face down on the sidewalk having to fend for ourselves. Satan is the father of lies, and this is his most destructive lie because it goes to the core of our identity.

The best way to combat a lie is to replace it with truth. The First Letter of John 3:1 tells us the truth of our relationship with God: "See what love the Father has bestowed on us in letting us be called children of God! Yet that is what we are."

In the Gospel of John, Jesus constantly talks about his relationship with the Father. "The Father and I are one" (Jn 10:30). "I am leaving the world and am going to the Father" (Jn 16:28). And my favorite verse: "I am not alone because the Father is with me" (Jn 16:32).

We are never alone. The Father is with us. The Father is with us even when we feel alone, isolated, flat on the pavement of life. The truth is *the Father is always with us.*

Jesus told a beautiful parable about our relationship with God the Father and how each of our lives is like a pilgrimage to the Father's house. It's the parable of the Prodigal Son in Luke 15.

I thought nothing more could be said about this parable until I attended a conference in Walsingham, England, in the summer of 2000. There, Bishop Joseph Ekuwem of Nigeria said that the parable of the Prodigal Son tells each of our stories because it tells the universal story of mankind.

Here's how he described it: At one point in time (before original sin), we lived in harmony with the Father (God) and the elder brother (others). We lived in the Father's house. Then, through our offense (original sin) we broke our relationship with the Father and went our own way.

However, despite our unfaithfulness, God has always been faithful. He constantly watches for us, expecting our return. When we return, the Father not only forgives us, but he also reconciles us to the family. This is the symbolism of the ring, robe, sandals, and festive celebration—it means the Father welcomes us back into the life of the family. Bishop Ekuwem stressed this important point: God the Father goes beyond forgiveness to reconciliation. The Father doesn't just forgive us and keep us at an arm's distance. He welcomes us back into the family. *He not only restores us to the same relationship we had with him before any offense, but also raises us to the status of adopted sons and daughters through the redemption Christ won for us.* The elder brother, however, goes ballistic. He's furious at his father for bringing his irresponsible younger brother back into the family with the same status and privileges.

But notice what the father says to the elder brother: "You are with me always." Frequently, this sentence slips by us, but it's the most important thing the father could have said! He's reminding the elder son (and us) that *the essence of fatherhood is not provision, but presence.* His fatherhood impelled him to welcome back his child not as a slave, but as a son, so he could be in the father's presence.

To the Father's House

This is where we need to find ourselves—in the Father's presence, in the Father's house. Not only have we been forgiven by the death of Jesus Christ, but we've been reconciled to God the Father. God welcomes us back not as a slave, but as a beloved daughter. Jesus Christ brings our relationship with God to a higher level than it was before any offense.

Take a moment and ask yourself: Do I experience my life as a journey to the house of the Father, a Father whose unconditional love has melted my heart so that I know I am his daughter?

Or am I struggling with my foundational identity, with my self-worth? Do I draw my identity mainly from mothering, from how well my children act at a restaurant, in church, at school, or when company comes over? Am I afraid others think poorly of me because of choices I make, or my husband makes, or because of family struggles with alcohol or addiction? Do I try to validate and prove my worth through my work, looks, or sexual relations?

Perhaps you're not married, and you feel you've been forgotten and ignored, that you're missing out on life because you're not a bride. Or maybe you're a widow or divorced, and you've been through the same wrenching I have, and you're not quite sure where to turn to reroot your identity. Or maybe you've been hurt, abandoned, or abused by your earthly father or another man and the thought of a heavenly Father does not console you, but frightens or repels you.

For all these reasons and more, it can be difficult for us to relate to God as Father, to know our foundational identity as a daughter.

We must beg God to bring us into his presence, to remove the faulty foundation of straw and hay in our lives and replace it with the one that will last forever.

Entering the Father's Presence

I invite you to take fifteen minutes in a quiet place and prayerfully read the following meditation. I suggest you close your eyes and begin with a short prayer asking the Holy Spirit to help you enter into a deeper relationship with your heavenly Father. Then, as you read through the meditation, stop and imagine the various scenes that are described. My prayer is that this will help you rediscover your identity as a daughter and begin the journey anew in the Father's presence.

Imagine yourself in the home you grew up in as a little girl. Look around, smell the familiar smells. See yourself sitting in the living room or family room as your father walks into the room (even if you never knew him). He stops, sees you, and walks over to you. He sits down opposite you, looks you in the eyes, and says to you, "How do you feel about me?"

You hesitate, not quite sure what to say, but then he says it again: "Really, how do you feel about me?" With that permission, you let the dam break and your hidden thoughts, pains, and fears come flooding out. What do you say to your father?

Now hear your father say back to you: "Is there anything else?" and you feel rise up within you the one thing you've always wanted to say to your father, but were afraid to. What is it? What do you want to say? You can say it to him now. It's safe. Tell him.

Now your father takes both of your hands and looks again into your eyes and says, "Tell me, my daughter, how have I failed you?" You look back at him, and the little girl inside you says: "Dad, you failed me when..." What do you say to him?

After telling your dad the things that hurt you, see him reach out and gather you into his arms and hold you close to his heart and say to you, "I'm sorry, I'm so sorry, my daughter. I had no idea how much I hurt you. If I had known, I never would have done that. I'm sorry, so, so sorry."

Now imagine yourself as that same girl in heaven. See yourself approaching the throne of God the Father. As you approach, the Father gets up and walks to meet you. He takes you by the hand and you walk up to the throne hand in hand, only you don't go up to the throne. Instead, you stop at the steps, and he sits down on the steps and invites you to sit beside him.

See the Father look at you and say, "Tell me, my daughter, how do you feel about me?" You hesitate, afraid to tell the King of the Universe what you really feel, but then he says, "It's all right. Tell me how you feel about me." What do you say to him? Hear yourself tell God the Father how you feel about him.

Now see God the Father take both your hands, bring you around in front of him, put you on his lap, and say to you tenderly: "Now tell me, how do you feel I have failed you?" It's safe. You're in the Father's house; you can tell him anything. There's nothing to hide. Tell the Father how you feel he has failed you.

Now hear the Father say, "Is there anything else you want to tell me?" What do you say to him? Pour your heart out to him.

When you're done, see the Father stand up, pick you up, and enfold you in his arms. Feel the warmth of the universe surround you and hear him say in your ear: "I'm sorry. I'm so, so sorry, my daughter, for all the pain and suffering you endured."

QUESTIONS FOR REFLECTION AND DISCUSSION

1. How would you describe your relationship with God right now?

2. Have you ever thought of yourself as a daughter of God? If this isn't your foundational identity, what is?

3. What prevents you from drawing closer to God as Father?

4. Take a moment and write a letter to God starting with "Dear Father." Write whatever comes to mind without censoring it.

5. Reflect on some places in Scripture that speak of God's tender love for us as his children, for example:

   1 John 3:1 "See what love the Father has given us, that we should be called children of God; and that is what we are."

   John 1:12 "But to all who received him, who believed in his name, he gave power to become children of God."

   Romans 8:14–17 "For all who are led by the Spirit of God are children of God. For you did not receive a spirit of slavery to fall back into fear, but you have received a spirit of adoption. When we cry, 'Abba! Father!' it is that very Spirit bearing witness with our spirit that we are children of God."

✥ CHAPTER 2 ✥

Why Male and Female?

REFOUNDING MY IDENTITY as a daughter of the Father was only the first chapter in rediscovering my feminine soul. As the years passed, I discovered I had more to learn.

Lady-in-Waiting

After my annulment, I assumed I would marry. I assumed I just had to maintain my little, part-time job until Prince Charming came along and rescued me.

There's a name for this mentality. It's called "lady-in-waiting," and I certainly had it. I was waiting for a man to come and rescue me from circumstances I hadn't chosen. I was waiting for a new romantic relationship to bring sparks and energy and purpose into my life. I was waiting ... waiting ... waiting ...

After a couple of years of waiting, I realized I was like a stalled car—all the potential to accelerate was there, but I wasn't moving. I had to jettison the marriage assumption and learn to walk in the weightlessness of single life. I had to decide what I wanted to *do* for the rest of my life to earn a living. *I had to learn what it meant to be a woman without a man.*

Before me was a smorgasbord of opinions. Books, talk-show hosts, and educational experts advised me to throw off the shackles of gender roles and remake myself as an autonomous "womyn," without reference to a man. But I wanted truth, not opinion. And I found that truth in the writings of Pope John Paul II.

John Paul II's teachings on women are innovative and time-less. He unveiled the deepest cry of a woman's heart with the tenderness and love of a bridegroom lifting the veil on his bride. Unfortunately, the media didn't usually portray him this way. More often they presented him as a cranky old celibate in Rome who wanted to keep women "in their place." Nothing could be further from the truth. John Paul II championed human dignity, and especially the beauty and dignity of women.

Same or Different?

In order to grasp the innovative nature of John Paul II's teachings, it's helpful to place him in context, to see him as a Rolls-Royce at the end of a long and complicated assembly line of philosophers and theologians. Fortunately, we don't have to review the entire 2,750-year history of thinking on women, because Sister Prudence Allen, RSM, has done a remarkable job in her two-volume set, *The Concept of Woman.*[1] Instead, we can look at just two ancient philosophers, Plato and Aristotle, and two Christian theologians, Augustine and Aquinas.

Plato's writings about women are surprising. He maintained there was no fundamental difference between women and men. He thought the soul was the true nature of the person, and because the soul was neither male nor female, women and men were essentially the same. True to his own teaching, Plato included women in his inner circle of students.

Aristotle occupies the opposite end of the spectrum. He thought men were naturally superior to women. He described the male as active, fertile, rational, and made to rule, while the female was passive, infertile, irrational, and made to obey. In short, Aristotle defined woman as an imperfect man.

While we can be indignant at pagan philosophers' ideas about the similarities and differences between men and women, Christian philosophers and theologians struggled with similar problems.

Following Plato's lead, Augustine said there was no difference between the soul of the male and female. However, in the physical world, he thought the female was a lesser image of God. Looking at her role as "helper," Augustine said the woman was more involved with the things of the earth, with the physical world, and this made her less spiritual and therefore less like God.

Good News and Bad

Finally, Thomas Aquinas heralded good news and bad news. The good news is that men and women are made equally in the image of God because both have an intelligent nature. For Aquinas, our ability to think rationally is how we reflect God most perfectly. Unlike animals, human persons have an intellect and will. This allows us to image God through reason and free choice.

Now for the bad news: Aquinas also thought that the male contained the image of God more perfectly than the female. In his interpretation of Genesis 2, Aquinas said the male received an immediate transfer of the divine image because he was created directly by God. This immediate transfer is absent in the female's creation because she was derived from the male.

I think of this as his separate-but-equal clause: male and female are equal because they are both rational creatures, but there's a hierarchy of perfection in which the male more closely images God than the female.

I'm afraid that if Aquinas or Aristotle were alive today they might be shredded to pieces, not just by radical feminists, but also by anyone who senses a devaluation of the feminine in favor of the masculine.

Mars ... Venus ... Earth?

As a result of this devaluation, our current age continues to be caught between two extremes. On the one hand, some women argue there are no real differences between male and female and so all legal and cultural differences should be wiped out. On the other swing of the pendulum, other women say the differences are fundamentally important and, in fact, women are superior to men.

This is where I found myself—smack in the midst of the gender battle. Are men and women the same or different? Is gender imposed on us by culture, or is it part of our being? Are men from Mars and women from Venus ... or from some other planet?

Fortunately, I didn't have to fight this battle on my own—John Paul II had entered the fray before me.

John Paul II spent years studying and meditating on the nature of men and women while he was earning graduate degrees in philosophy and theology. As a parish priest, he counseled married couples and even went on camping trips with them. As pope, he spent hours in prayer before the Eucharist and at the altar. The fruit of his life's work is a new synthesis of thought concerning this age-old debate about men and women.

To dig out John Paul II's new synthesis, we have to go back to the first years of his pontificate. In September 1979, less than one year after his surprise election as pope, John Paul II began a series of teachings based on Genesis 1 and 2.

In these teachings, John Paul II systematically presented the meaning of male and female as made in the image and likeness of God. These teachings were originally published in a little book called *Original Unity of Man and Woman*, but have been republished in a larger collection entitled *Man and Woman He Created Them: A Theology of the Body*,[2] or more simply, the "theology of the body."

Original Unity of Man and Woman is like uranium—compact and dense, yet powerful. It contains the nucleus of John Paul II's teachings about the dignity of men and women. Through these teachings, John Paul II introduced new terms such as "spousal meaning of the body," "original solitude," "original nakedness," and *communio personarum* (the communion of persons).

This is what makes John Paul II both difficult and rewarding to read. By developing new language, he attempted to capture spiritual realities in human words. It's as if John Paul II were looking through the microscope of faith and trying to describe dimensions of the human person previously hidden from sight.

Back to the Beginning

With John Paul II as our guide, let's look through the microscope of faith. Let's go back to "the beginning," back to Genesis 1 and 2 in order to take a new look at what Scripture teaches us about the nature of men and women.

In Genesis 1:27 we read: "God created man in his image; in the divine image he created him; male and female he created them." This truth captivated John Paul II's life and thought. *Everything in his theology of the body attempts to understand how both male and female are made in the image and likeness of God.* And to penetrate the depth of this reality, John Paul II focused the microscope on Genesis 2 and the second account of creation.

In this account, male and female are not created at the same time. Instead, Genesis 2:7 tells us, "the Lord God formed man out of the clay of the ground and blew into his nostrils the breath of life, and so man became a living being."

Genesis 2:7 reveals something new about the human person: We are more than the material world, more than clay of the ground. We are also breath or spirit. (In Hebrew, the word for breath, *ruah*, also means spirit.)

Unique Creation

This is an important point. In all creation (that we know of) only human persons are this unique combination of matter and spirit. Animals aren't this combination because they're only matter. Angels aren't this unique combination because they're only spirit. Only human persons image God by being both body and spirit for, as John Paul II said, man "belongs to the visible world while going beyond it."[3]

Let's jump ahead a few verses to Genesis 2:18–20. In these verses, God decides to make a suitable partner for Adam, but none can be found. Adam is alone.

If we stop and think for a moment, we realize Adam really isn't alone. God, birds, cattle, and flowers fill this earthly paradise, and yet Adam experiences himself as alone. This is because no other creature is made in the image and likeness of God in the same way he is. Adam is alone because only Adam is both body and spirit.

No Longer Alone

How does God solve Adam's solitude? God casts Adam into a deep sleep, takes a rib from his side, and forms it into a woman. Upon waking from sleep and seeing the female, Adam gushes: "This at last is bone of my bones and flesh of my flesh; this one shall be called 'Woman,' for out of Man this one was taken" (Gen 2:23).

Immediately, Adam recognizes (finally!! hallelujah!!) another being who shares his same nature. Scripture could have said: "And God put Adam to sleep and fashioned another human being for him, ho hum ... (yawn)," but it doesn't.

Showing Equality

As I learned in writing class, *show* don't *tell*. Scripture is *showing* us a fundamental truth: Men are not from Mars and women are not from Venus. *They're from the same body.* For John Paul II, this establishes the absolute equality of male and female. Men and women are equal because we come from the same body. We share the same nature.

Up to this point, Genesis 2 is carefully guiding us through a profound visual journey:

1. Adam is made of clay and breath (body and spirit);

2. Adam is alone;

3. Adam is still alone even after the creation of the animals;

4. God solves Adam's solitude by creating Eve from the side of Adam, from the same body.

Made for Communion

This creation journey is a carefully crafted symphony moving toward a crescendo, the crescendo of Genesis 2:24: "That is why a man leaves his father and mother and clings to his wife, and the two of them become one body." This is a crescendo of union: of marital union certainly, but more fundamentally of interpersonal communion.

Genesis 2:24 is a crucial verse for John Paul II. It reveals the deepest essence of the human person. We are not made for solitude, but for communion. In fact, John Paul II proclaimed that "man becomes an image of God not so much in the moment of solitude as in the moment of communion." [4]

This is his new contribution to 2,700 years of philosophy and theology—that the human person images God not only through his rationality, as Aquinas thought, but even more fundamentally through his ability for union and communion. [5]

A Tango Lesson

I love to dance Argentine tango, and, as is often said, it takes two to tango. The same is true of imaging God: it takes two to image God. If we only imaged God through our rationality, one would have been enough. Adam would have been sufficient.

But he wasn't. Just as it takes two to tango, it takes two to image God. Male and female image God *together*.

Now, if you're not married, you're probably ready to chuck this book and think you've been left out again. No, a thousand times no. Every person—young, old, single, married, with children, and without children—images God by living in interpersonal communion. Marriage is the original expression of this interpersonal communion, but it's not the only one (read on...).

The Spiral

One of the most difficult aspects of John Paul II's thinking and writing is his spiral style. Most novels, history books, and magazine articles are written in a linear way. They have a beginning, middle, and end that progress in a straightforward manner. But that's not how John Paul II wrote. He writes about something, goes away from it for a while, and then revisits it on a deeper level. Instead of expecting John Paul II to always say something new, expect him to go deeper.

We can see this spiral pattern in his writings on imaging God. Yes, we image God "not so much in the moment of solitude as in the moment of communion," but, as John Paul II wrote elsewhere, "To say that man [i.e., person] is created in the image and likeness of God means that man is called to exist 'for' others, to become a gift."[6] For John Paul II, the key word is "gift." *We image God by making a sincere gift of self.*

Why is this point stressed?

To answer that question we have to fast-forward from Genesis to the New Testament and Jesus' revelation about the inner life of God. Jesus revealed that God was not only One, but Three. God is Trinity.

Unfortunately, the word "Trinity" often lacks visual content in our minds other than a triangle or Saint Patrick's shamrock. When I think of God as Trinity, here's how I like to image it: *The Father pours himself out in gift to the Son. The Son pours himself out in gift to the Father, and the Holy Spirit bursts forth as the fruit of their self-giving love.*[7]

God is one nature, but in that one nature the Father and Son pour themselves out in gift to each other, and that gift is not sterile but fruitful. It bursts forth as the Holy Spirit.

Trinitarian Reflection

Here's the really exciting part: As human persons, we are one (human) nature, but we are also two—male and female—and so we can pour ourselves out in gift to each other. And that gift is meant to be fruitful.

God is a union and communion of fruitful, self-giving love. So, too, as human persons we are called to live in a union and communion of fruitful, self-giving love. If we live this way, others will be able to see God, the Trinity, through us and our self-giving.

God designed the family to be a human trinity in time and

history. He designed the love of husband and wife to burst forth in the fruitfulness of children. But he also designed the love between parent and child, friend and friend, aunt and niece, and widow and grandchild to be spiritually fruitful (more about this in chapter 3).

The Divine Design

John Paul II loved to meditate on our ability to make a sincere gift of self, to self-donate. The male/female distinction is not culturally imposed or an evolutionary accident. It's the divine design. Male and female emerge from one human nature in order to pour themselves out in gift to each other, a gift that's designed to be fruitful, a gift that involves the whole person.

If we spiral back to the beginning of this chapter and ask again, "Are male and female the same or different?" the answer is "both." We're the same because we come from the same body and share the same nature, and we're different because we're male and female. Many of the male/female differences (both charming and maddening) have been catalogued by John Gray in his Mars and Venus books.[8] His insights have helped thousands of people understand why men and women think and act differently.

However, difference is only half the equation. Precisely because we're different *and the same* we can we live in a union and communion of fruitful, self-giving love. Precisely because the Persons of the Trinity are distinct *and the same* the Trinity can exist in a union and communion of fruitful, self-giving love.

Body Basics

These ideas may be difficult and at times jolting because they seem new and somewhat abstract. However, they're actually very concrete. Everything is based on the human body, on asking why God made us male and female, not male and male or female and female.

The reason is union. When we look at the male and female body, we can't help but notice that they go together, that they are made for union. This bodily reality opens our eyes to a spiritual reality—the reality that we are made for union and communion with God and others through a sincere gift of self.

Old Expressions Aren't Enough

John Paul II coined a new expression to describe this interpersonal reality of union and communion. He called it the "spousal meaning of the body." This was his innovative way of saying, "The body is made for union."

What is true of your body, however, isn't *just* true of your physical existence. It is true also of your whole person. Your body expresses your person. It expresses who you are. Your entire being is made for spiritual, emotional, psychological, and interpersonal union.

One Way to Happiness

John Paul II considered the spousal meaning of the body, *your* body, to be the fundamental personal reality of your existence in the world. It is what orients you to a communion of persons. In other words, if you don't realize you're made for union and communion through a sincere gift of self, you'll seek other sources of happiness. When this happens, our bodies are no longer the source of deeply personal and satisfying communion, but of frustration, hollowness, and pain (more about this in chapter 4).

Simplifying JP2

When my son was 10 years old, I tried to explain the spousal meaning of the body to him at the dinner table. After seeing his puzzled expression (I can't imagine why), I devised a shorthand way of explaining it: *"We're made from one nature, embodied in two ways, for the purpose of union and communion through a sincere and fruitful gift of self."*

This description is worth committing to memory. It can change the whole way we view ourselves, others, and God. It can remind us constantly of how and why we were created as male and female: to be a gift. This truth defined Pope John Paul II's life. As women on the journey, we're invited to do the same.

QUESTIONS FOR REFLECTION AND DISCUSSION

1. What strikes you about the views of Plato and Aristotle? What about those of Augustine and Aquinas?

2. Before reading this chapter, would you have said men and women are the same or different? Why?

3. What strikes you in John Paul II's description of male and female as created from the same body? Does this change the way you view yourself and/or others?

4. Have you ever felt the loneliness Adam experienced where you couldn't "connect" with the world around you?

5. Do you agree or disagree with John Paul II's statement that the human person becomes the image of God "not so much in the moment of solitude as in the moment of communion"? Why?

6. Have you ever thought of yourself as a reflection of the fruitful, self-giving love of the Trinity?

7. Can you recall the description of the spousal meaning of the body without looking at the previous page?

⊰ CHAPTER 3 ⊱

The Feminine Genius

EINSTEIN WAS A GENIUS. Beethoven was a genius. Michelangelo was a genius. Each of them had a unique ability to bring into being something that never existed before.

Women, too, have a creative genius. We have the unique ability to bring into being something that never existed before. To capture this unique ability, John Paul II coined a new term, the "feminine genius." Rather than discounting women or recasting them in the image and likeness of men, John Paul II wanted to affirm the feminine way of doing things, to highlight the distinctive way a woman makes a gift of self.

The Real Meaning of "Helper"

In speaking about the feminine genius, John Paul II broke new ground. While Augustine said woman's role as "helper" meant she was more bound up in the physical world, John Paul II's theology of the body takes a different route: Man, "after having become completely conscious of his own solitude among all the living beings on the earth, awaits a 'help similar to himself' (see Gen 2:20). None of these beings (*animalia* [animals]), in fact, offers man the basic conditions that *make it possible to exist in a relation of reciprocal gift.*" [1]

A bit later, he continues: "... 'alone,' the man does not completely realize this essence [of being made in the image and likeness of God]. He realizes it only by existing '*with someone*'—and, put even more deeply and completely, by existing '*for someone.*'" [2]

The Gift of Woman

For John Paul II, being a "helper" doesn't refer to the practical things of life like cooking, cleaning, and caring for the kids. It means the woman helps the man discover his own humanity, his own capacity for relational self-giving.

Here's how I visualize it: Woman's first presence in the world was as gift. God created her and presented her as gift to man. By being gift to him, she showed him how to make a sincere gift of self. She revealed to him the spousal meaning of his own body, that he was made for union and communion through a sincere gift of self.

The uniqueness of woman is awesome. Without her, the male cannot realize the meaning of his existence—to exist with and for someone. Nor can he understand fully what it means to be a person, to be created in the image and likeness of God for a sincere gift of self. Without her, the task of life is simply to care for the garden (i.e., to earn a living). But with her, man learns the meaning of life as union and communion through a sincere gift of self.

This explanation of the genius of women may work for the garden of Eden, but what about today? Am I suggesting women show up on the doorstep of eligible bachelors with bows on their heads and say, "I'm your gift!"? (Let me know if it works.)

The Empty Space

To help others understand the meaning of life as union and communion, God has given us a very concrete answer: the feminine body. The feminine body is radically different from the masculine body. For starters, we have curves, more connectors between the two sides of the brain, and less muscle mass. But there's another way the feminine body is different. Only women are created with an empty space within.

Women are created to be receptive, to be life-givers. A woman's entire being is oriented toward receiving and nurturing new life. We make a gift of self so that others can receive the gift of self, their very life.

The feminine genius indeed brings into being something that never existed before—a new human life. Far from being abstract and impersonal, the feminine gift of self is concrete, intimate, and highly personal. It involves the union of a woman's body with the child within.

In his apostolic letter, *On the Dignity and Vocation of Women*, John Paul II reflected on this feminine gift of self: "Motherhood implies from the beginning [i.e., before original sin] a special openness to the new person.... In this openness ... the woman discovers herself through a sincere gift of self." And in the next paragraph he adds: "Motherhood is linked to the personal structure of the woman and to the personal dimension of the gift."[3]

The very way a woman's being is knit together is for a sincere gift of self through motherhood. The feminine genius is meant to be creative and *pro*creative.

Another Kind of Motherhood

But what about women who aren't mothers? Are they somehow excluded from the genius of women, from this feminine gift of self?

Not for a moment! Once again John Paul II spirals deeper by introducing another facet of a woman's being—that of spiritual motherhood. I like to think of the nature of woman as a sparkling diamond that John Paul II held up to the light of faith. As he turned it this way and that, he admired the diamond and continued to describe the different ways it reflected the light.

I might have been blind to this feminine facet of spiritual motherhood for my whole life if it hadn't been for an unusual romantic relationship.

Several years ago, I began dating someone whose spirituality was from Eastern mysticism. For four months, God put me through a crash course in ecumenism and evangelization. As we explored our different spiritualities, I had to articulate what I believed about the cross, self-sacrificial love, redemption, and birth control.

In the process, I realized that while my explanations about the faith could till the soil of my friend's heart, ultimately he needed to experience the person of Jesus Christ.

While we continued to discuss "the issues," I vowed to go to Mass on the days we would see each other. In this way, I could receive Jesus into my body and then imitate Mary by bearing Christ to my friend through Jesus' eucharistic presence within me.

I could be a Christ-bearer. I could bring Christ to my friend in a way that transcended our differences and disagreements, and hopefully would penetrate his heart rather than just his intellect. That, I discovered, was the easy part.

One summer day, I had the privilege of praying with Babsie Bleasdell. Babsie is a dynamic preacher of the word from Trinidad, West Indies, who has a grandmotherly and maternal heart. She was visiting Steubenville to speak at a conference, so I seized the opportunity to get together and pray about my relationship with my Eastern mystic.

After we prayed, I was driving to meet him and I heard in my spirit, "Pray to convert your romantic love into a maternal love." Needless to say, my first response was, "No way!"

Over the years, however, I've learned that whenever I'm resisting the Spirit, I should pray for the grace to be *willing* to pray for whatever is being asked of me. So I started praying: "Holy Spirit, help me be *willing* to pray to convert my romantic love into a maternal love."

Within two days my heart was changed, and I was praying sincerely to convert my romantic love into a maternal love. But then I had to ask, "What is a maternal love?"

The answer came to me unexpectedly a couple of weeks later as I was parking my car at work. I was sitting behind the steering wheel when suddenly I realized that maternal love is the way I love my son, Michael: it is constant, unconditional, and doesn't expect my emotional needs to be met in return. My love for him does not go up and down; it does not depend on whether he is good or bad. Nor do I expect him to care for my emotional needs.

Spiritual Motherhood Defined

I didn't realize it then, but the Holy Spirit was tutoring me in spiritual motherhood. In fact, it wasn't until I read John Paul II's *Letter to Women*[4] and *On the Dignity and Vocation of Women* that I discovered the name for what I was doing—it is called *spiritual motherhood, and it means nurturing the emotional, moral, cultural, and spiritual life of others.*

Once I understood this, I began to realize that I could express spiritual motherhood in countless ways: smiling at someone in the grocery store, praying with my son on the way to the bus stop, teaching dance to senior citizens, making a meal for someone who's just had a baby, listening to a friend on the phone, and, my favorite way: giving roses to my women friends.

As I talked to other women and looked at their lives, I noticed they, too, were being spiritual mothers, often without realizing it. For instance, a friend named Patty, who is single, fiftyish, and a guidance counselor, is devoted to her students. She helps them know every educational, professional, and technical opportunity available to them. And because she is single, she considers whomever she is working with to be her family, to be the people God has given her to nurture and to care for their well-being.

Patty puts it this way: "I'm not a mom, but that's okay because I have a lot of other titles: aunt, friend, godmother, guidance counselor, sister, and cousin. I try to be another hand of God on earth, to be there when people need me and to be generous with my time and love." Patty's grasped the heart of spiritual motherhood.

Then there's Maureen. She married a faithful, loving Christian man, and within a year Maureen was staying at home with their newborn son, Andrew. Then the script started to change. When her son was two years old, he was diagnosed with autism. Day after day she had to deal with a hyperactive boy who flipped the lights on and off, who dumped toys in a huge pile in the middle of the floor and left them there, and who was still potty training at age five.

But Maureen learned to see Andrew with her heart. She learned to value his eternal destiny rather than getting frustrated over his earthly limitations. As a spiritual mother, she sees with her heart.

Finally, there's Mary Lou, who graduated from college in 1950 but didn't have the stereotypical '50s marriage. Her husband owned a small grocery store where Mary Lou worked eight hours a day, five or six days a week. Yet even in the midst of her busy life, Mary Lou provided a glue, a cohesiveness, that bonded her family of four children together.

Dinner time was sacred in her house—no running to soccer practice or out for a meeting. Every night Mary Lou cooked dinner, and every night the six of them gathered around the table to catch up on the day. This was the way Mary Lou nurtured the emotional, moral, and spiritual life of her children even in the midst of working.

Everyday Heroism

Examples of spiritual motherhood abound, both among the saints and ordinary people. John Paul II called this type of living "everyday heroism." A significant part of this everyday heroism, he said, is the "silent but effective and eloquent witness of all those 'brave mothers who devote themselves to their own family without reserve, who suffer in giving birth to their children, and who are ready to make any effort, to face any sacrifice, in order to pass on to them the best of themselves.'"[5]

In fact, John Paul II emphasizes that biological motherhood must be completed by spiritual motherhood. He notes this precise point in his apostolic letter, *On the Dignity and Vocation of Women*, in which he writes: "And does not physical motherhood also have to be a spiritual motherhood, in order to respond to the whole truth about the human being who is a unity of body and spirit?"[6]

As is evident from human experience, merely giving physical life to a child isn't enough. We must form and direct the emotional, moral, cultural, biological, and psychological life of our children as well. This is what makes biological motherhood so incredibly demanding: it doesn't end with giving birth, it just begins!

Of course John Paul II's beautiful description of the brave self-giving of biological mothers applies to all women who give of themselves in the workplace, church, neighborhood, and extended family. All women are called to give birth—physically and/or spiritually. All women are called to be Christ-bearers, to receive divine life in the womb of their souls and bear Christ to the world. All women are called to see in Mary's spiritual motherhood a reflection of their own lives.[7]

If all women embraced the call to spiritual motherhood, they would ignite a nuclear reaction that would spread the culture of life through the whole world. The feminine genius would set the whole world on fire!

Every Woman's Call

It makes sense, then, that while some women are called to biological motherhood, *every woman is called to spiritual motherhood because motherhood is knit into the very structure of a woman's being.* Women are created with the gift of interior readiness to receive others into their lives, and in doing so, to nurture their emotional, moral, cultural, and spiritual well-being.

This is an exciting and creative challenge because women can be spiritual mothers anywhere: in the office, at home, with their grandchildren, in the neighborhood, even sick in bed.

A spiritual mother can be single, married, or widowed. She can have ten children or no children, work in the home or out of the home. In fact, I find many women have already discovered this part of the journey. They're already being spiritual mothers without realizing it. They just didn't have a name for what they were doing.

But I'd like to give a word of caution. When I first started speaking about spiritual motherhood, women thought I was telling them to be doormats, to let everyone walk all over them and to have no boundaries.

That's *not* what I'm saying. *Spiritual motherhood is not an indiscriminate gift of self* as if a woman has to give and give and give to whoever asks of her. A spiritual mother helps others grow into wholeness, not dependency. She nurtures the emotional, moral, cultural, and spiritual life of others so they can make a fuller gift of self to God and others, not so they can be irresponsible and self-indulgent. Sometimes the best thing a spiritual mother can do is to say no.

Open Wide the World to Women

Liberating the feminine genius is the passionate cry of John Paul II's messages to women. He was convinced that biological and spiritual motherhood could rebuild a civilization of love and a culture of life. That is why he said:

> It is necessary to strive convincingly to ensure that the widest possible space is open to women in all areas of culture, economics, politics, and ecclesial life itself, so that all human society is increasingly enriched by the gifts proper to masculinity and femininity.[8]

Like leaven in the dough, the genius of women must bring its uplifting presence into the boardroom, courtroom, and classroom. Unceasingly, John Paul II pleaded for political and social change in order for women to fully share their gifts with the whole community and to be artisans of peace.[9]

Open Wide the Church to Women

Increasing women's participation in public and political life is only one-third of John Paul II's message to women. He also appealed to the whole Church community to "foster feminine participation in every way in its internal life."[10]

Just so we could understand the extent to which he expected the Church to foster this feminine participation, John Paul II enumerated the possibilities:

> I am thinking, for example, of theological teaching, the forms of liturgical ministry permitted, including service at the altar, pastoral and administrative councils, diocesan synods and particular councils, various ecclesial institutions, curias, and ecclesiastical tribunals, many pastoral activities, including the new forms of participation in the care of parishes when there is a shortage of clergy, except for those tasks that belong properly to the priest.[11]

(More about women and the priesthood in chapter 8.)

Open Wide the Home to Women

But we must not misinterpret John Paul II. Promoting the presence and participation of women in all aspects of society and the Church should never be at the expense of the family. The importance of the family comprises the final third of his message.

The challenge facing most societies, he said, "is that of upholding, indeed strengthening, woman's role in the family while at the same time making it possible for her to use all her talents and exercise all her rights in building up society."[12]

A mother's presence in the family must be recognized, applauded, and supported, he reminded the world, while the misconception that motherhood "is oppressive to women, and ... prevents a woman from reaching personal fulfillment, and ... from having an influence on society" must be dispelled.[13]

Changing Culture

John Paul II often taught and wrote from a both/and position. We see this especially in his writings on women. He implored women to live out the feminine genius in the home *and* in public life *and* in the Church. Why all three? Because ultimately it is culture—the context in which we live life—that must change. And that context includes the home, the Church, and society.[14]

This is why John Paul II constantly called us to rebuild a culture of life and a civilization of love. He urged the whole body of Christ to develop a culture that affirms women's dignity and respects and welcomes femininity. Gender is not something to be eliminated. It is to be celebrated and accentuated.

More than ten years ago, John Paul II invited women to "reflect carefully on what it means to speak of the *'genius of women,'* not only in order to be able to see in this phrase a specific part of God's plan which needs to be accepted and appreciated, but also in order to let this genius be more fully expressed in the life of society as a whole, as well as in the life of the Church." That invitation is even more urgent today. Every woman is given the task of reflecting on her own feminine genius so as to unlock its spiritual dynamism for the Church, the family, and the world.

Defining the Feminine Genius

Although John Paul II never formally defined the feminine genius, I would describe it this way: *The feminine genius is the distinctive way a woman expresses her gift of self in all her feminine fullness and originality, as God intended her to be from the beginning. The feminine genius is the "active" and "external" expression of her "being."*

As women, we must not be swallowed up by a culture that tells us there's no real difference between men and women, nor can we succumb to a society that demeans women for their feminine distinctiveness. Rather, let us always keep in mind that every woman's journey is to live her feminine genius in an original and unique way, so as to bring into being that which never existed before—human life, spiritual life, and the fullness of emotional and cultural life.

QUESTIONS FOR REFLECTION AND DISCUSSION

1. Before reading this chapter, what was your impression of John Paul II's view of women? Did your view change?

2. What do you think is the unique way a woman makes a sincere gift of self?

3. Have you ever thought of yourself as a spiritual mother? Why or why not?

4. How can you make spiritual motherhood a part of your everyday life?

5. How would you define the feminine genius?

❧ CHAPTER 4 ❧

Sin and the Spousal Meaning of the Body

A COUPLE OF YEARS AGO, I gave a talk on the spousal meaning of the body at a parish in Pennsylvania. Afterward, editor and writer Mike Aquilina sent me a cartoon portraying a surprised priest being confronted by an unfriendly customs official. The caption read: "That's right, Father. I said strip—right down to the spousal meaning of your body."

This was obviously a well-informed (but fictional) customs official. For most of us, the spousal meaning of the body isn't a household word. When was the last time someone asked you, "So, how's the spousal meaning of your body today?" We don't talk this way. Something happened on the journey between the "beginning" and today, and that something was original sin.

In his writings, John Paul II not only delved into the "genesis" of the human person (our creation in the image and likeness of God) and the feminine "genius" (the way women make a distinctly feminine gift of self), he also addressed the "gouging" we've received as a result of original sin.

GO NY!!

To reflect on this gouging, John Paul II turned to the story of original sin in Genesis 3. In this story, Satan tempts Eve not only with a sin of the intellect and emotions (to be like God), but with a sin of the body. He tempts her to eat the fruit and so involve her body in the first sin of mankind.

This is not a minor detail. Original sin indeed darkens the intellect and disorders the emotions, but it also ruptures our ability for union and communion through the body on four levels. These four levels of union are what the *Catechism of the Catholic Church* calls the four harmonies[1] and what I like to call "GO NY!!"

G = God

Sin ruptures our union and communion with *God*. When God shows up, Adam and Eve hide because they're afraid. John Paul II described the change in relationship this way: "Man turns his back on God-Love, on the 'Father.' He in some sense casts him from his heart."[2] At the end of Genesis 3, we see the ultimate rupture in our relationship with God: Adam and Eve are cast out of the garden, out of God's presence (3:23).

O = Others

Sin ruptures our union and communion with *others*. When God asks Adam if he's eaten from the tree, he commits the original blame shift: "The woman whom you gave to be with me, she gave me fruit from the tree" (Gen 3:12). Eve, in turns, blames the serpent. And the pattern goes on ...

The rupture between man and woman is also highlighted in the consequences pronounced by God. He tells Eve, "Your desire will be for your husband and he will lord it over you" (Gen 3:16).[3] This foretells how some women will sacrifice their dignity for the sake of male attention and security, and how some men will use this desire to their advantage.

John Paul II likewise recognized this rupture: "[A]fter the breaking of the original covenant with God, man and woman did not find themselves united with each other, but rather more divided or even set against each other because of their masculinity and femininity."[4]

N = Nature

Sin ruptures our union and communion with *nature*. Every woman who labors to give birth ("in pain you shall bring forth children," Gen 3:16) and every man (and woman) who labors to earn a living ("by the sweat of your face you shall eat bread," Gen 3:19) experiences this rupture.

Whereas God designed us to be fruitful in harmony with nature ("Be fruitful and multiply; and fill the earth and subdue it," Gen 1:28), original sin introduced tension and conflict into our relationship with the created order. Fruitfulness won't happen without suffering. Here's how John Paul II described this conflict: "The words of God-Yahweh foretell the hostility, as it were, of the world, the resistance of nature against man and his tasks."[5]

Y = *Yourself*

Sin ruptures the union and communion between body and spirit. This is evidenced by the birth of shame. Adam and Eve cover their bodies not because they have a sudden hankering for designer fig leaves, but because they feel exposed. Instead of experiencing the body as a sign of their self-giving union, the body is seen as an object to be used.

The body is clothed not because the body is bad, but because the body no longer radiates the spirit. Acknowledging the body/spirit split, John Paul II wrote: "These words reveal a certain constitutive fracture in the human person's interior, *a breakup, as it were, of man's original spiritual and somatic [bodily] unity*. He realizes for the first time that his body has ceased drawing on the power of the spirit."[6]

No Private Affair

Once again, Scripture is showing (rather than telling) a profound truth: our ability for union and communion through a sincere gift of self has been ruptured. While Genesis 1 and 2 guide us on a visual journey of life "in the beginning," Genesis 3 provides a visual journey of life ruptured by sin. Through this journey we see that sin is never an individual affair. It profoundly affects the way we relate to God, to others, to the world around us, and even to our own bodies.

After sin, the body no longer leaps at the opportunity to make a sincere gift of self for union and communion, but leans toward the temptation to live apart from God's design. The traditional term "concupiscence" means exactly this: our "leaning" or "inclination" toward sin. As John Paul II observed, we are pulled "toward the appeasement of the body, often at the cost of an authentic and full communion of persons."[7]

In the journey of life we, too, are subject to this pull. Satan remains an ever-present foe, targeting our feminine bodies just as he targeted Eve's. As a result, Satan tempts us again and again to sin in the body. If he can rupture our ability for union and communion through the body, then he's on his way to destroying the image of God in us.

Satan's Five Strategies

When it comes to women, Satan has at least five favorite strategies to tempt women to sin in the body and thus to dismantle and destroy the feminine genius. I like to call these the inferiority syndrome, the counterfeit-union syndrome, the 7–10 split syndrome, the freedom-from syndrome, and the appendix syndrome.

1. The Inferiority Syndrome

First, *the inferiority syndrome*. Many women have been bluntly told in school, the workplace, or even their own family that they were unwanted because they weren't born a boy or that they're inferior because they're not male. This message gets embedded into their self-concept, and for these women, the body is not a source of joy and delight, but of pain and shame. This is also true for women who have been abused physically and/or emotionally by their fathers or men they trusted, or who have been neglected or abused by their mothers.

Burying the Body

Due to pain and shame, many women take their femininity and bury it deep in the ground like a coffin, hoping it will never resurface. Some women masculinize their bodies by adopting male standards of success, dress, and even loose morals to prove their "equality" or worth. Other women purposefully gain excessive weight to make their bodies ugly and undesirable.

John Paul II warned against masculinizing our bodies when he reminded women: "In the name of liberation from male 'domination,' women must not appropriate to themselves male characteristics contrary to their own feminine 'originality.' There is a well-founded fear that if they take this path, women will not 'reach fulfillment,' but instead will *deform and lose their essential richness*." [8]

In order to unmask Satan's masculinizing strategy, it's helpful to consider where we may have buried our feminine side because of pain and shame, or copied masculine ways of thinking and acting in order to compete or prove our worth. In doing so, we may have neglected the particular way we image God's presence in the world, which, John Paul II says, is our sensitivity to what is personal and relational.

2. The Counterfeit-Union Syndrome

But being relational isn't always easy, which brings us to the second way Satan tempts women through their bodies—*the counterfeit-union syndrome*. Because women are structured in their being for union, we yearn for intimacy with another, sometimes at the sacrifice of our own dignity and identity.

As a result, we're tempted to use our bodies for counterfeit union.

The insidious thing about a counterfeit is that it looks like the real thing, smells like the real thing, and can even be used like the real thing. But it's not the real thing. It's a counterfeit.

When the FBI trains its agents to spot counterfeits, they study the real thing intensively. By exposing agents to what is authentic and genuine, counterfeits are more easily identified. The imitation pales in comparison to the real thing.

Settling for Second Best

Unfortunately, many women are willing to settle for imitation intimacy. We use our bodies for counterfeit union through sexual relationships outside of marriage, cohabitation, homosexual acts, and contraceptive use. While growing numbers of people struggle with same-sex attraction and attempt to grapple with its psychological and cultural causes, there's another side we must not forget—the spiritual side. One of Satan's most effective strategies to obscure God's design for the body is to distort the profound gift of physical union and procreative fruitfulness between a man and a woman. God designed us to image the Trinity by being one nature embodied in two ways, for the purpose of union and communion through a sincere and fruitful gift of self. Difference allows for fruitfulness.

In a homosexual union, sameness (male/male or female/female) is preferred over difference. This "union" can never burst forth in the fruitfulness of a child, but remains sterile. Homosexual acts and all false intimacy have this sterilizing effect. They encourage the counterfeit union of two individuals rather than the real communion of two persons. And tragically, where this occurs the feminine genius can become obscured altogether.

Fashioned for Union

Often I ask myself, "Why are women so tempted by counterfeit union? Why do we remain in abusive and compromising situations?"

Our culture tells us it's because we love too much or because we're from Venus. Hogwash! It's because women are structured in their being for union and communion. The union of egg and sperm takes place within a woman's body. The unborn child is united to its mother through the umbilical cord. The newborn infant receives its nourishment by being connected to its mother's breast.

However, because original sin wounds the spousal meaning of the body, women often don't know how to express their desire for union and intimacy other than in a romantic or sexual way.

Intimacy or Romance?

One of the biggest mistakes women make is *confusing intimacy with romance*. We think they're the same thing, and they're not. I might have gone my whole adult life confusing the two if it wasn't for Argentine tango.

One night, I danced a wonderful tango with a man. As the song ended, I remained in his arms with a warm, melted chocolate feeling. My thoughts drifted toward the ozone layer and thoughts of romance when I said to myself, "Time out, Katrina, you know this man! Off the dance floor he's arrogant and self-centered, and never asks you how you are. How could you even consider being romantic with him?"

That night taught me one of the most important lessons of my adult feminine life: the difference between intimacy and romance. Intimacy (for women) is the feeling of emotional closeness, of being safe, secure, and accepted in another's space. But romance is different. Romance moves toward an exclusive and permanent relationship with another that involves the total gift of self.

As women, we need to learn how to experience emotional closeness as a dimension of being made for union and communion while realizing it doesn't give us the green light to race into romance.

Women are created for emotionally intimate friendships. Otherwise we shrivel up and die. We become parched like a desert and then, when a trickle of male attention comes our way, we soak it up. Before we know it, we're knee deep or waist deep or over our heads in counterfeit union.

Emotional Counterfeit Union

For married women, counterfeit union can take on an emotional dimension as well. If a married woman shares her intimate thoughts and feelings with a man who is not her husband, she can bond with him in a way that replaces or competes with her emotional marital bond. What began as an "innocent friendship" diverts more and more of a woman's emotional attention from her spouse to this emotionally nourishing relationship.

Because the physical dimension isn't involved, it can be harder to recognize the "friendship" as a transgression against

the marital bond. Yet it is. Women in these situations must
sever the competing relationship, despite the wrenching pain
it will cause.

What, then, is a woman in an emotionally barren marriage
to do? Does she cut off all contact with men? Does she grit her
teeth and embrace a life of emotional martyrdom?

No, but she does have to turn to her feminine friendships
to provide a sense of being cherished, of being connected and
bonded with another.[9] Women have a much greater RDA
(*Relational* Daily Allowance) than men.

I know it sounds trite, but one man can never supply all of
a woman's relational needs. Not only that, one friendship can
never supply all of a woman's relational needs. We need
friends to go shopping with, friends to pray with, friends to
hike with, and friends to cry with.

If we truly want to avoid counterfeit union, whether as
married or single women, then developing feminine friendships must take center stage. As we do so, it will be easier and
easier to make the distinction between intimacy and romance,
and so avoid the hurtful trap of Genesis 3:16: "Your desire will
be for your husband [i.e., a man] and he will lord it over you."
And we can help our friends avoid this trap as well.

Starving for Union

Some women may never be tempted by counterfeit sexual
or emotional union. Instead their desire for union finds a different avenue for expression: addiction.

A woman's craving for union and intimacy is so strong that
when it goes unmet, it can pop up through addiction or other
unhealthy attachments. Alcoholism, eating disorders, depres-

sion, self-stimulation, even workaholism and bodybuilding can be feminine attempts to numb or fill this unmet need for intimacy.

But don't get obsessive about this. Just because a woman craves chocolate or buys a new couch doesn't necessarily mean she's starved for union. Still, it's worth looking at why women eat when they're upset, go shopping when they feel a gnawing emptiness inside, or find themselves overcommitted. A woman's inability to say no, whether to food, a garage-sale bargain, alcohol, or volunteering, often has its roots in her intense, but usually subconscious, desire for union and communion.

3. The 7–10 Split Syndrome

Unfortunately, modern culture doesn't help women understand and integrate this desire for union and intimacy very well. Instead, it helps Satan bombard women with his third attack: *the 7–10 split syndrome.*

If you've ever gone bowling, you've probably experienced the 7–10 split. This happens when you roll the ball, hit the head pin smack in the center, and end up with the 7 pin on one side and the 10 pin on the other side.

This is what Satan wants to do with us. He's constantly hitting us on the "head pin"—hitting our minds and emotions to get the body on one side and the spirit on the other. He wants us to forget the body has any spiritual meaning, and to think the body is just … a body.

Woman or Object?

How does he do this? Turn on the TV. Look at billboards. Read *Cosmopolitan.* Pick up a romance novel. Watch MTV.

(Okay, *don't* watch MTV.) Television, music, advertisements, and movies often completely ignore the spiritual dimension of a woman. Rather than portraying women as spiritually alive and open to new life within the covenant of marriage, pop culture zeros in on the physical dimension. This reduces women to objects to be used for sexual gratification and pleasure apart from God's design.

John Paul II was keenly aware of this reductionist approach: "It is, in fact, one thing to be aware that the value of sex [i.e., sexual relations] is part of the whole richness of values with which a feminine being appears to a man; it quite another thing to 'reduce' the whole personal richness of femininity to this one value, that is, to sex as the fitting object of the satisfaction of one's own sexuality."[10]

Only Matter

Even scientific experts contribute to the 7–10 split. They assume the body is mere biology, just a highly evolved collection of molecules and organs that keeps you breathing, walking, talking.

If the body has no deeper spiritual significance, then you have every right to do with it whatever you want. In this view, in fact, it would be *irresponsible* not to use birth control or sterilization to control your fertility. After all, if science and technology have figured out a way to do it, then why not?

If your body was just biology, this would be true. You could do whatever you want with your body or whatever you want with someone else's body. It would be a fine use of science and technology to cut up, tie off, and take out healthy parts of the body since it's only matter.

More Than Biology

But we're not just biology. We're not just matter. We're human persons who image God through body and spirit. It really matters what you do with your matter! Despite what the media, science, and well-meaning people in the Church have said, contraception, sterilization, abortion, and *in vitro* fertilization are not blessings of modern technology. They are part of Satan's plan to split your body from your spirit, to reduce you and your body to merely the physical dimension.

A Sacred Sign

In God's design, *a woman's body and her fertility are not just biology; they also have a spiritual reality*. The feminine body is designed by God to be a sacred sign, to reveal God. A woman's body, mind, spirit, and fertility together image the Trinity—the fruitful, self-giving love of the Trinity.

A Sterile God

Contraception, abortion, and sterilization project a different image of God to the world—a sterile image. The love between the Father and Son no longer bursts forth in the fruitfulness of another Person, but is self-contained. God is not a fruitful Trinity, but a sterile duality. The Holy Spirit is contracepted out of the Trinity. The procreative genius of woman is put on the back burner or eliminated altogether. The sexual act is reduced to its physical dimension.

The 7–10 split syndrome makes a contraceptive, anti-woman culture possible. It barrages us with a view of reality in which it's perfectly acceptable to split the body from the spirit, to make the other into an object for our pleasure. Sadly, this split allows women to be used in the marital covenant and outside of it, to have all the personal riches of her femininity reduced to a single value.

To Be Loved or to Be Used?

In the midst of all this, God's message can be difficult to hear and absorb. It calls for a change, and few of us like to be asked to change. God, however, never demands. He invites. He appeals to our hearts and minds and, most of all, to our dignity and free will. *God wants all women to be loved rather than used*. He wants our journey to be one of reuniting body and spirit into a life-giving whole rather than dividing ourselves into disconnected, sterile pieces. He desires the sacred reality of the feminine body and its ability to image God to be the source of true happiness and freedom. He wants us to discover the fullness of our feminine genius.

4. The Freedom-from Syndrome

Redefining happiness and freedom is precisely the goal of Satan's fourth strategy: *the freedom-from syndrome*.

Have you ever noticed that freedom in the media is usually portrayed as a "freedom from"? Freedom from responsibility and housework; freedom from Church rules; freedom from fat, wrinkles, and old-age spots. This type of unrestricted freedom, the media promises, will make you happy.

In the Service of Love

It's funny how we rarely hear about the freedom *to*—the freedom to love unconditionally, to suffer without bitterness, to not compare ourselves, to make a sincere gift of self. This type of freedom refuses to make itself into an absolute. It always places freedom in the service of love. The goal of Christian freedom is not more freedom, but love. It's love that makes us happy, not unrestricted freedom.

Perhaps you might like to take a moment and ask yourself: What does freedom mean to me? Am I tempted to think of freedom as getting rid of restrictive rules and regulations? Do I dream of happiness apart from pregnancy or housework? Do I think getting a better-paying job or a bigger house will bring me real freedom? Am I waiting for the day I lose thirty pounds or Prince Charming rescues me from the single life?

These struggles are real, and yet the answer is not fully found in "freedom from." It's found in the freedom *to* encounter God and make a sincere gift of self even before you lose thirty pounds or as you trudge to work day after day. It's the freedom to live passionately even before Prince Charming arrives, or to welcome an unexpected child. It's the freedom to love in the midst of imperfect and unanticipated situations.

5. The Appendix Syndrome

And finally, Satan uses a fifth strategy: *the appendix syndrome*. In reaction to society's obsession with sex and physical appearance, many Christian women go to the opposite extreme and overspiritualize. We downplay our bodies.

How many of us have been tempted to think, "Oh, if only I could get rid of my body, I'd be more holy!" We can't wait to shed the body like a snake's skin and leave it behind at death. We think the soul is what truly images God, and the body is unnecessary, like an appendix. We're tempted to think our identity wouldn't really change if the body were removed. In fact, we'd be better off without it!

Saving Souls

Unfortunately, this thinking has crept into our spiritual language. For instance, I often hear the expression, "Jesus came to save souls." Actually, he didn't. Jesus came to save *persons*. As Christians, we believe our salvation will not be complete until soul and body are united with the Lord forever in heaven. Jesus came to save you as a person, not just a soul without a body. So get used to your body; it'll be with you for all eternity!

Heavenly Bodies

Recently I spoke with a friend about her parish discussion group's reaction to this last comment. Many of the women were puzzled. They didn't understand what I meant about our bodies going to heaven with us. They thought the body returned to ash and remained ash, as if it were just temporary housing. End of discussion.

I'm reminded again how many Christians misunderstand the body. If the body is just temporary housing, it doesn't matter if we ignore it, starve it, sterilize it, or excessively pierce it. In fact, it doesn't even matter if it's male or female. After all, some day we'll be rid of it and then we'll finally be free.

Not Generic

Jesus didn't get rid of his body. It was glorified. And in that glorified state, it was still *his* body. His wounds remained. He said to Thomas, "Put your finger here and see my hands.

Reach out your hand and put it in my side. Do not doubt but believe!" (Jn 20:27). Our glorified body will be *our* body, not someone else's body or a generic body. *Somehow our resurrected body will resemble the body we have on earth.*

What does the glorified body look like? No one knows for sure, but when responding to this question, Paul wrote to the Corinthians: "There are both heavenly bodies and earthly bodies, but the glory of the heavenly is one thing, and that of the earthly is another.... What is sown is perishable, what is raised is imperishable.... It is sown a physical body, it is raised a spiritual body" (1 Cor 15:40, 42, 44).

The glorified and natural body are the same and different. As John Paul II said many times, the body expresses the person; it expresses the spirit.[11] We image God by being both body and spirit. This is true on earth *and* in heaven, even though in heaven, body and spirit are transformed in a completely new way.

The Body Reveals God

The process, however, of transforming our bodies into spiritual ones begins even now. We've all seen or met someone who radiates the Spirit. People flocked to Blessed Teresa of Calcutta (Mother Teresa) because they experienced God's presence through her. John Paul II lived only to glorify God in his body even while his body was ravaged by Parkinson's disease and compromised by slurred speech.

The work of salvation on earth is not getting rid of our bodies, but allowing God to be revealed ("glorified") through our bodies. Jesus, the Second Person of the Blessed Trinity, revealed God by taking on flesh. The Gospel of John says it so clearly: "The

Word became flesh and lived among us, and we have seen his glory, the glory as of a father's only Son" (Jn 1:14). Jesus tells his disciples: "Whoever has seen me [i.e., my body] has seen the Father" (Jn 14:9).

The same is true of us. We "take on flesh" so that we can reveal God. In Paul's words: "Do you not know that your body is a temple of the Holy Spirit within you ... therefore glorify [reveal] God in your body" (1 Cor 6:19–20).

How to Image Body and Soul

Cathedral of the Soul

If, then, we're suppose to befriend our bodies even on this earthly journey, how is that possible? Here's the way I love to image the relationship between body and soul: *the soul is the tabernacle of the body, and the body is the cathedral of the soul.*

We would never place a tabernacle out in the open, exposed to everything around it. Likewise, it would be impossible to have a cathedral without a tabernacle because it would no longer be a sacred space. The tabernacle needs the cathedral, and the cathedral needs the tabernacle. The two go together. So, too, the soul needs the body, and the body needs the soul. They go together.

Eucharist of the Body

A second image I love is that of the monstrance and the Eucharist. The monstrance is a beautiful holder used for eucharistic adoration, often in the shape of a sunburst. The Eucharist is placed at its center. Using this image we could say *the body is the monstrance of the soul, and the soul is the Eucharist of the body.*

The purpose of the monstrance is to display and enhance the beauty of the Eucharist. Likewise, the purpose of the body is to display and enhance the beauty of the soul. They don't compete with each other. They *complete* each other to bring out their shared beauty and brilliance.

In order to heal the effects of sin and resist Satan's strategies, we have to start here—with the cathedral of our bodies. Many women struggle with their identity as daughters and as women precisely because they struggle with their bodies.

We need the grace to love and reverence our bodies, not just to tolerate them. We need to understand that we image God through the body. And most importantly, we have to be healed of the shame, self-hatred, addiction, and hurtful memories that prevent us from living in union and communion with God, others, nature, and within ourselves between body and spirit.

Our God is not only a saving God, but also a healing God. He's deeply aware of our feminine wounds and our intense need to be loved and accepted. He wants to bring us close to his wounded side, to cleanse our memories, and to heal the gaping wounds that ravage our hearts.

Saint Paul says, "If anyone is in Christ, there is a new creation: everything old has passed away; see, everything has become new!" (2 Cor 5:17). Every woman's journey must pass through the loving gaze of the Father as well as the grace of the cross. Our entire being is meant to be born again from the wounded side of Christ. The Christian journey is not only the redemption of the spirit, but also the redemption of the body. This is what frees us to live our feminine genius to the full!

Healing Body and Soul

To end this chapter, I invite you to find a quiet place and pray the following meditation:

Lord, I come to you this day and ask you to renew my life. Take me into the womb of your heart so that I may be reborn from the side of Christ. As you rebirth me into the world, may the water and blood that flowed from your side wash and purify my memory, emotions, understanding, and will. May it strip away the anger, hurt, and resentment encasing my heart toward those who have ridiculed, rejected, or abused me because of my femininity.

Please remove every feeling of self-despising, condemnation, and self-rejection embedded within me and replace them with a peace and acceptance of who you made me to be from the beginning.

Lord, I repent for trying to satisfy my desires for union and intimacy through counterfeit union or sexual relations outside of marriage. You know how much I long to be one with another! I give these longings to you and ask you to satisfy them. I am sorry for the times I've allowed my body to be used as an object, for failing to stand up for my own dignity, and for betraying my unique ability to give life.

Please send your Holy Spirit to liberate me from Satan's strategies that would blind me and distract me from my feminine genius and thus my true dignity and vocation as a woman in the world.

Lord, I want to reveal you through my body. Help me to come forth from your side with all the beauty and purity of a bride adorned for her wedding, so that I can be the temple of the Holy Spirit you created me to be. Thank you, Jesus, for loving me and coming to re-create me right now, at this moment, in this place.

QUESTIONS FOR REFLECTION AND DISCUSSION

1. How have you experienced sin disrupting your ability to make a sincere gift of self to God and others?

2. Have you ever struggled with any of the five syndromes: inferiority, counterfeit-union, 7–10 split, freedom-from, or appendix? Are there other ways you've struggled with your body?

3. Does the image of a cathedral and a tabernacle, or a monstrance and the Eucharist, help you understand better the relationship between body and soul? Can you think of another image to describe this relationship?

4. What areas in your life need to be reborn from the side of Christ?

❦ CHAPTER 5 ❧

Weaving a Tapestry of Life

LIVING THE FULLNESS of womanhood is tough. As we have seen in the previous chapters, we have to recover our identity as daughters of the Father, be awakened to the feminine genius, and be healed of the wounds that paralyze and misshape our feminine identity. We might be tempted to think the journey is over. And yet, the journey pushes on.

Living in Process

Once when my son misbehaved, I ripped into him like a chainsaw cutting into a tree. He fled crying to his room while I sat in the kitchen tormented by guilt, remorse, and failure. Unexpectedly, the Holy Spirit slipped a thought into my heart: "The process is just as important as the end product."

In that moment, I realized I could stampede my son into acting the way I wanted, but to what avail? The *process* of disciplining him was the real arena where values and virtues were passed on.

This insight not only changed my interactions with my son, but it also changed my life. I began repeating to myself: "The process is just as important as the end product." Soon, even that paradigm had to shift when God showed me: *"The process is the end product."*

I had to stop racing toward the future or pining for the past. I had to live in the present moment and love the journey (a journey that ultimately, of course, leads to eternal life). I find it difficult to love the journey. I'd much rather arrive than be on my way. However, that pesky fly from chapter 1 won't let me "arrive." I keep finding myself asking, "Who am I?" because who I am at eighteen is different from who I am at twenty-five, or thirty-five, or sixty-five, or eighty-five. The journey continues. The Holy Spirit beckons on. So, what's next?

Having been married for ten years, I agonized when my marriage failed and I had to redefine myself as a single person. It felt so awkward. I didn't fit in with single people because I had a family. I didn't fit in with married people because I didn't have a husband.

Not only that, but shortly after my marriage failed, the Catholic community around which everything in my life had been woven as a seamless garment was also wrenched in two.

Suddenly, everything wasn't so neatly connected. In fact, my life had splintered into fragments—the fragments of work, parish life, and what was left of community life; the fragments of cooking, housecleaning, mowing the lawn, and paying bills; the fragments of my son's school, redefined relationships, and single parenting. Rather than a nice, tidy seamless garment, I had a disconnected patchwork quilt.

It was humbling. With the shoe of divorce on my foot, with our exalted Catholic community brought low, my pride took a deadly blow. I used to think, "Look at my life—with a little more effort and self-discipline, you can do it too." Now I was simply hanging on for dear life, trying not to come apart at the seams because I was pulled in so many different directions.

The patchwork-quilt stage went on for about four years as I collected pieces and tried to find ways to bind them together. During this time, an important piece of the quilt came to me from Dr. Ronda Chervin, a Catholic woman philosopher in the United States. She introduced me to another Catholic woman philosopher, Saint Edith Stein, a Carmelite nun who died in a Nazi concentration camp and was canonized in 1998 by Pope John Paul II.

U-G-I

In her essays on women, Edith Stein described three levels of vocation.[1] First, every person has a universal vocation (U), a vocation shared with all people. Secondly, we each have a vocation according to gender (G), whether we are male or female. And thirdly, we have an individual vocation (I), one that is uniquely ours.

When I learned about these three vocations, the pieces of my fractured life started to make more sense. It was like turning a kaleidoscope and having the pieces fall into place to make a pattern. And, in fact, these three vocations provide the framework for this book.

Daughter of the Father

Our first vocation, the universal vocation we share in common with everyone, is that we are children of God. This is what God showed me on my thirtieth birthday when he told me I was first a daughter, then a bride. Chapter 1 explored our universal vocation by reflecting on a woman's foundational identity as a daughter of the Father.

The Genius of Woman

Our second vocation is our vocation according to gender. Chapters 2 and 3 focused on this vocation. In these chapters we saw how women are created for union and communion through a feminine gift of self. We are created with an empty space within, to be receptive, to be life-bearers. Motherhood is knit into the very structure of our being. This means every woman, single or married, is called to maternity—emotional, moral, cultural, and spiritual maternity. This is a woman's second vocation.

Uniquely What?

But what about the third vocation, that vocation which is uniquely ours? Because my life was composed of competing patchwork squares as mother, writer, friend, cook, dancer, teacher, maintenance man, and so forth, I felt parceled out. None of these "roles" encompassed me fully.

When I began to look at my life as three levels of vocation instead of just one, I was greatly relieved. I didn't need to have one, grand, all-encompassing vocation for my life to make sense. I could operate out of the first two levels as a daughter of the Father and as a woman, while waiting for God to reveal the third level.

What about this third vocation? What's an intelligent single mom like me to do? More of the answer came to me in a most unexpected way.

Snow Lessons

One October, I decided to sell my minivan and buy a compact car. I paid for the compact with my credit card, giving me two months to sell the minivan and pay off my card. No problem.

That October weekend it started snowing, and it didn't stop for five months. When it snows in my part of Ohio, nobody shops for a car. We hibernate in our warm houses and drive as little as possible. When Christmas rolled around, I still had two cars and a significant credit card debt. It was time for Plan B.

I contacted two of my sisters, who have comfortable living standards, and requested to borrow $1,000 and pay it back in six months. In response, they accused me of financial irresponsibility, poor planning, and living beyond my means.

I was shocked, hurt, and demeaned. However, their reactions launched me on an extensive self-examination: Was I being irresponsible? Unreasonable? Was I failing to plan for my financial future? Why didn't I have more money? What was important to me now and in the future?

As I thought about my situation and my sisters' comments, I realized that my sisters, both being scientists, value what can be measured, what can be seen. I, on the other hand, place greater value on what is intangible—listening to a friend,

walking my son to the bus stop, teaching confirmation class-
es, leaving a cheerful note for a co-worker.

My life was poured out not on those things that could be
measured and therefore prove that I had used my time respon-
sibly, but on enriching the lives of others and helping them
carry their burdens. To me, intangibles were so much more
important than tangibles. This added one more piece to the
already complicated patchwork quilt I felt my life to be. Now
that I understood how important the intangibles were to
me—things such as friendship, wholeness, spiritual growth,
and emotional nourishment—what did I do with these? And
how did I reconcile this with all the other demands on my life?

Opposites Go Together

I was bemoaning my situation to a priest one day, and he
introduced me to a concept that Saint Bonaventure called the
coincidence of opposites. I like to call it the coexistence of
opposites. It's simple and it goes like this: Within ourselves we
experience opposite desires and traits. We experience a desire
for union and for independence, to be among people and to be
alone, to be generous and to be self-protective, to be patient
and to act impulsively. We experience both transcendence and
limitation.

According to Bonaventure, this is the way we're created,
with this coexistence of opposites. I kept thinking something
was wrong with me because I had all these "competing"
desires: I am a Christian, and I love to dance tango. I love
nature, and I love the city. I love philosophy, and I love flag
football. I love to travel, and I have to mow the lawn. I'm a
mom, and I'm a wage earner.

I thought I had to choose one side over the other, one extreme over the other. With this new insight of the coexistence of opposites, I realized it wasn't an either/or situation but a both/and. I can love the transcendent and live in the concrete. I can value the intangibles and appreciate the tangibles.

Born Again, a Tapestry

I came away from that meeting with a new view of myself. I felt reconstituted, born again on the inside. I suddenly realized I no longer felt like a patchwork quilt. Now my life was a beautiful tapestry, with each thread expressing a different part of who I am, woven together to make a beautiful picture.

I also realized something else. Whenever I thought of my life as a seamless garment, I'd always pictured it as a solid, burlap brown. When I thought of the patchwork quilt, it was squares of color pasted together, but making no overall picture. Now, as a tapestry, I could imagine beautiful oranges, vibrant reds, rich peacock blues. *And the contrasts among the different colors were precisely what made the tapestry beautiful.*

For the first time, I began to welcome contrast in my life, without feeling as if I had to make everything the same. I can love the universal and the concrete. I can be fully alive as a Christian and pursue my love of dance. I can be a single mother and a wage earner. I can live in the city and love nature. The internal war was over and both sides had won. Hallelujah!

My Uniqueness

It may seem like I've gone far afield, but actually this relates to my unique vocation. Through this process of selling the van (which sold after six months to someone who wanted to buy it the first month, but couldn't), I learned how I am put together on the inside, how God has uniquely created Katrina Zeno: I live for the intangibles, for that which can't be measured in dollars and cents as demonstrated by a well-furnished home or a high job position.

But I also learned that the concrete is very important. I have to learn to love the concrete because it is through the concrete—through a hug, a beautiful sunset, an exquisite dance, a homeless person—that we encounter the intangibles. As a friend of mine delights in saying, "I'm changing the world one diaper at a time."

Weaving a New Life

What does this mean for you who have journeyed with me from a seamless garment to a patchwork quilt to a colorful tapestry? It means that you, too, have a beautiful tapestry inside yourself, waiting to be discovered. God wants to take what might seem like a jumbled life of carpooling, housework, professional responsibilities, homeschooling, wage earning, and elderly parent caretaking and weave it into something beautiful.

God wants to reawaken dimensions of your life you've either discarded because you're a wife and mother or disregarded because you're *not* a wife and mother. He wants to give your whole self back to you. He's inviting you to love the spiritual and the concrete.

Some of you reading this are probably nodding your heads and saying, "Yes, yes!" Others may be scratching your heads and wondering what the fuss is about. It's this: after our children are no longer young or we've toiled in the professional world for fifteen or twenty years, we find ourselves asking again, "Who am I?" That pesky fly returns to question whether our value and identity go deeper than the roles we play or the functions we perform. Otherwise we would be replaceable cogs in the grinding gears of the universe.

If being a replaceable cog disturbs you, I applaud you. You've sensed what John Paul II loved to say about each of us: that we are unique and unrepeatable. You are unrepeatable. There's no one else like you in the world. No one else can fill your shoes. No one else was born at this time in history with your particular gifts, temperament, and life experience. You have a unique vocation. You are a unique tapestry. You are not a replaceable cog.

The challenge, of course, is realizing that this unique vocation doesn't mean we're going to be famous or celebrated. Most often it means we'll live hidden, uncelebrated lives. Who ever hears of the woman in Magadan, Siberia, struggling to feed her children, or the woman professor in Slovakia teaching Christian psychology? Yet, each life is a unique strand in the divine tapestry, an indispensable part of the beauty of creation, whose absence would leave a gaping hole.

One Person Makes a Difference

A story I heard recently reconvinced me of each person's value and the unique contribution we make to the divine tapestry. In the early twentieth century, a poor family in Poland had two sons. Both sons wanted to be priests, but the family only had enough money to educate the older son to serve the Church. One day the mother, who was a midwife, needed some medicine for a patient, but the local pharmacist had run out. The younger son ran all the way to a pharmacist in the next town to ask for the necessary medicine.

When this pharmacist saw the young boy's willing spirit and spark for life, he inquired about his family and future desires. The boy confessed he wanted to be a priest, but the family couldn't afford his education. The pharmacist instructed the boy to go home and tell his parents that he (the pharmacist) would be willing to teach the boy Latin and the other necessary subjects without charge.

This is precisely what happened, and the boy became Saint Maximilian Kolbe: the Franciscan priest who inspired millions through his love of Mary and by giving his life in exchange for that of another prisoner in the Auschwitz concentration camp.

Lifetime Endeavor

Saints and tapestries are made by using the ordinary events of daily life. Likewise, our unique vocation unfolds in this same way, through the ordinary (and sometimes not so ordinary) events of daily life. Our unique vocation isn't a do-it-yourself kit that we discover one day, assemble, and finish. Our unique vocation unfolds throughout our lifetime.

Events, hardships, broken hearts, hidden talents, joys, and gifts all conspire to keep our life flowing around the next bend. Sometimes the current is calm; other times it's turbulent. Some stretches are shallow, others deep. Sometimes the scenery bursts forth in awe-inspiring mountains; other times it reveals scruffy oaks and barren patches.

Through it all, one thing in life is predictable: change. Not only that, things change and change again. Change, however, isn't arbitrary. God allows the stretching, fracturing, and reconfiguring of our lives in order to weave our unique tapestries in a more holistic (and holy) way.

For me, the most astonishing fact about our unique vocation is that it continues even in heaven. Our personal uniqueness will not be absorbed in heaven, John Paul II assures us, but will stand out to an incomparably greater and fuller extent.[2]

Wow! Who we are as unique and unrepeatable persons is accentuated in heaven, not diminished. This compels me to take my uniqueness seriously, to develop my human and artistic talents as absolutely necessary to the journey of my salvation and that of others.

Living the Process

As I've tried to live this process of embracing my unique vocation, three thoughts have struck me:

1. Running on Empty

One of the greatest obstacles to unfolding our unique vocation is exhaustion and depletion. It's impossible for a woman's uniqueness to unfold if her emotional interior is dry or she feels the needle is pointing way past empty.

The experience of exhaustion and depletion is the most common complaint I hear among women with small children or those who are working full time and raising a family. I think we'd be overspiritualizing if we ignore these feelings. So how do we remedy the situation?

From Channel to Reservoir

One way is to change the way we view ourselves. I used to think of myself as a channel through whom grace flowed to others. I kept nothing for myself. I was simply a conduit. Then I heard that Saint Bernard of Clairvaux wrote that we should be reservoirs that pour out of our overflow.

If we're called to be reservoirs, we have to be replenished in order to continue giving out of our overflow. If nothing flows into the reservoir, it's only a matter of time before we're empty and barren.

Unfortunately, many of us walk around empty and depleted because of guilt—not real guilt, but false guilt. Real guilt convicts us when we have acted wrongly, when we have sinned against God and others.

False guilt is a nagging voice that tells us we should be doing something else. It doesn't reveal objective wrongdoing, but accuses us of being unproductive and self-indulgent. It pops up when we choose stillness over activity, "no" over "yes," receiving over giving.

Coming Out of Hibernation

Here's the challenge: if we really believe God has a unique vocation for us, that we've been given a unique personality and gifts and have been born at this time in history for a reason, then we need to allow this uniqueness to unfold.

We need to slay false guilt and give ourselves permission to ask: How am I uniquely created? What are my personal interests and gifts? What replenishes me? Do I like to ski, garden, play the piano, play tennis, read a book? Am I interested in politics, counseling, natural medicine, or calligraphy? What were my dreams as a young girl? What talents or gifts have gone into hibernation?

More Than a Role

Even just asking these questions often provokes twinges of guilt and sighs of impossibilities. The days are crammed with rushing kids off to school, rushing to work, rushing to get dinner ready. The Holy Spirit must convince us that developing who we are as unique persons *apart from the roles we play* is honoring who God made us to be. It's reawakening our unique vocation from its midlife slumber.

So be creative. Put your feminine genius to work. See if you can figure out common interests with your husband, children, roommates, or friends to find things that uniquely express who you are. Over the years, my son and I have danced, gone horseback riding, and played cards and games together. I've attempted street hockey (I don't recommend it), basketball, and playing catcher for his fastball (ouch).

If you don't share common interests with your husband, children, or roommates, figure out ways they can make a sincere gift of self to you by freeing an hour or two a week for the things that replenish you.

I know this is hard for most women, and it even feels unnatural. Women find it excruciating to ask others to sacrifice for them. We'd rather inconvenience ourselves than inconvenience others.

However, please remember you are asking others to make a gift of self to you not so you can be self-indulgent, but so you can make a richer and fuller gift of your *unique* self back to God, your family, friends, and the world. A friend loves to describe the life of women in this way: We get filled up and we get poured out. As women, most of us are experts at the pouring out part; I'm simply asking you to be more deliberate about getting filled up.

2. Productivity Versus Fruitfulness

As you begin embracing more of your unique vocation, you may find the Holy Spirit changes your thinking from being productive to being fruitful.

Checklist Value

Most of us are familiar with being productive. We constantly evaluate our days according to how many things we checked off our checklist or PDA. If we checked off a lot, we had a good day. If we checked off only two or three items, it wasn't such a good day. I think God has a different vision by which he wants us to view ourselves, and that's the vision of fruitfulness.

This became apparent to me in May 1998 when I left my job as a publications writer for Franciscan University of Steubenville in Ohio. I felt I needed to resign so I could pursue my unique vocation as a speaker and writer of Catholic spirituality. I grappled with this decision for almost two years because of my need to provide for my family and my past experience of appearing "irresponsible."

Fruitfulness of the Spirit

That same month, I read a book on the Blessed Mother by Marie-Dominique Philippe, OP, in which he described the Holy Spirit choosing Mary as his spouse to act in fruitfulness with her.[3] I couldn't keep reading. I had to put the book down and let that sentence convert me. The Holy Spirit was moving in my heart, telling me he wanted to do the same with me. He wanted to act in fruitfulness with me.

Not surprisingly, John Paul II echoed this same thought: "Only Mary and Joseph, who lived the mystery of [Jesus'] birth, became the first witnesses of a fruitfulness different from that of the flesh, that is, the fruitfulness of the Spirit."[4]

Linear Versus Spiral

This led me to reflect further on the difference between productivity and fruitfulness. Most of my life I've been very productive. This implies a linear idea of progress—a beginning, middle, and end that's accomplished in a straightforward sequence. At the end, something tangible and measurable is produced, which didn't necessarily require the cooperation of others to accomplish.

Fruitfulness is different. It is a hidden process, one that is spiral rather than linear. Sometimes it takes a while for fruitfulness to take shape because nothing visibly emerges at first.

Fruitfulness also implies the cooperation of others. We're not fruitful by ourselves. A plant doesn't produce fruit by its own efforts but through a combination of factors. When a fruit matures, it isn't usually weighed and measured, but simply admired and appreciated.

A Different Standard

This is how I'm trying to look at my life now—that God is calling me to be fruitful. If at first my efforts don't seem to produce anything measurable, that's okay. In fact, it may take a while for the fruit to mature, but that doesn't mean I'm being irresponsible or nonproductive. It just means I'm being fruitful.

I'd like to give one word of warning: Living a fruitful life is tough! It's countercultural. It takes fortitude and perseverance because most people don't understand fruitfulness according to the Spirit.

Threefold Healing

Yet fruitfulness according to the Spirit is incredibly healing. It spills over into each of the three vocations Saint Edith Stein wrote about: Living our unique vocation heals the rupture between body and spirit. Living our vocation as women heals the rupture between us and others. And living our vocation as a daughter of the Father heals the rupture between us and God.

I can see this happening in me now. As I embrace more fully my unique vocation, I no longer experience a disconnect between who I am and what I do. More and more, they are the same thing. At times, I experience an incredible oneness of body and spirit that is so freeing, passionate, and full of life that I want to shout with Saint Symeon the New Theologian: "I see how I was and what I have become. O wonder!"[5]

3. O Fiat!

Finally, to end this chapter, I'd like to turn to Mary and her unique life call. The Swiss theologian Hans Urs von Balthasar wrote: "Mary opens up countless possibilities of saying 'yes' for all who come after her. All of them are personal, all of them are original; according to God's commission, all of them are new and have never existed before.... For the Christian, above all else, is a man [woman] who says 'Yes.'"[6]

By saying yes to God, Mary was faithful to her unique vocation. She opened up new possibilities for realizing God's plan of salvation. She fully lived her feminine genius, and history was never the same.

Your Fiat Counts

The same is true for each of us. God is writing an original script with each of our lives. He's not writing a remake or adaptation of someone else's life, but something never before written. Through each of us, God wants to open up countless possibilities of saying yes for all who come after us. *Never underestimate the power and fruitfulness of your "yes" to God!*

Daughter, Woman, Unique Tapestry

If, then, we combine everything we've reflected on so far, a woman is first a daughter of the Father. This is her universal vocation.

Second, she is created to make a feminine and sincere gift of self to others, especially through spiritual motherhood. This is her vocation according to gender.

Finally, every woman is entrusted with a unique vocation, a beautiful tapestry composed of a variety of colors and contrasts that is woven throughout the course of her life using her unique circumstances, struggles, gifts, and talents. Through her unique yes, she opens up countless possibilities for fruitfulness through the Holy Spirit.

The Master Weaver

Our unique tapestry is a creative endeavor. It's also a mystery and tribute to God's sovereignty and self-giving love. On the one hand, we are filled with hope. On the other hand, pain and suffering stretch our faith beyond human limits, and we want to cry, "Lord, I believe. Help my unbelief!" (cf. Mk 9:24).

I am indebted to the unknown author of the following poem, who captures in a surpassingly elegant manner everything I've been trying to say. As you read it, may you sense the Master's hand weaving together the threads of your life.

The Plan of the Master Weaver

Our lives are but fine weavings
that God and we prepare,
each life becomes a fabric planned
and fashioned in his care.
We may not always see just how
the weavings intertwine,
but we must trust the Master's hand
and follow his design.
For he can view the pattern
upon the upper side,

while we must look from underneath
and trust in him to guide ...
Sometimes a strand of sorrow
is added to his plan,
and though it's difficult for us,
we still must understand
that it's he who fills the shuttle,
it's he who knows what's best,
so we must weave in patience
and leave to him the rest ...
Not till the loom is silent
and the shuttle ceases to fly
shall God unroll the canvas
and explain the reason why—
the dark threads are as needed
in the Weaver's skillful hand
as the threads of gold and silver
in the pattern he has planned.

QUESTIONS FOR REFLECTION AND DISCUSSION

1. Which image do you most identify with at this time in
    your life: seamless garment, patchwork quilt, or tapes-
    try?

2. Is there another image you would use to describe your
    life at this moment (for example: mosaic, garden, bat-
    tered car, empty glass, chalice)? Why?

3. How does the concept of three vocations change the way you look at your life?

4. Do you have a sense of what your unique vocation might be?

5. What prevents your uniqueness from unfolding?

6. Are you able to replenish the reservoir periodically, or is it more often depleted?

7. Do you evaluate yourself more according to your productivity or your fruitfulness? Would you like to change this standard of evaluation? How?

8. How would you answer the question "Who am I?" at this point in your life?

≈ CHAPTER 6 ≈

The Spouse of the Spirit

WOVEN INTO EVERY WOMAN'S unique tapestry is an incredibly strong yearning for intimacy and union. This thread accounts for the peaks and valleys of most women's lives.

When a woman feels close to someone, she feels alive, energized, and valued. When she feels alienated and isolated from others, life can be a living hell. Simple tasks are draining. Her emotional pulse is flat. She wonders whether the journey is even worth living.

Obviously we don't experience mountaintop intimacy every moment of our lives. But does this mean we aren't living in union with God and others? Is it possible to live moment-by-moment union even when we don't live perpetually on the mountaintop?

Beyond Daughter

When God showed me in 1991 that I was first a daughter, then a bride, the bride part had no meaning beyond being someone's wife. I merely thought God was refounding the core of my identity as a daughter of God before any-thing else.

This was certainly true, but God's word to us often has lay-ers of meaning. Perhaps you've experienced reading a Scripture verse you've heard many times before and suddenly it leaps off the page. The verse has new meaning because your life circumstances have changed.

It sounds noble to say "forgive your enemies" or "nothing is impossible for God," until unforgiveness hardens your heart or you can't conceive a child because of infertility. Then Scripture takes on new power and new authority, and some-times we feel it's written just for us.

The same can be true of spiritual insights—words, phras-es, or images we receive in prayer. For years, I focused exclu-sively on the daughter part of "first a daughter, then a bride" ... until the summer of 1997.

High-flying Romance

That summer I was flying high ... literally. I'd met a man who danced Argentine tango and who lived 500 miles away in Massachusetts. Four out of five weekends I flew to Massa-chusetts to nurture this blossoming romance. And what a wonderful romance it was!

We went hiking, inline skating, sailing, and camping. We danced tango and sipped wine while sitting in his hot tub look-ing at the stars. I felt alive, free, and passionate again. I no longer felt as if I carried the burden of my life alone. I began dreaming of the possibility of a future together, and for the first time in years, I allowed my romantic love to be stirred up.

Then the plane crashed ... figuratively. Just before I left for a three-week trip to Buenos Aires, he broke the news: although he loved me, he couldn't see a permanent future for us because of our religious differences. He thought it better to break off the relationship now rather than cause me more pain later. More pain? My heart couldn't absorb the thought; it was already numbed by pain. I cried. He cried. We both cried, and I got on the plane to Ohio to endure the agony of a bleeding heart alone.

Over the next two months, I tried to be brave. I tried to get my heart to neutral, to convince myself of all the reasons why our relationship wouldn't work.

Instead, I kept discovering all the reasons why our relationship should continue. Now all of that was being wrenched away from me, and my heart was bleeding. I wanted to bandage my heart, to bind it up, to make it stop bleeding and take away the hurt.

Broken and Open

Then one morning I realized my heart wasn't just bleeding, it was broken. This man had broken my heart. It hurt so much to admit it. But in that moment of admitting it, the Holy Spirit showed me something else. The Spirit showed me that Jesus, too, had a broken heart, and it was from his broken heart on the cross that God's love and mercy flowed.

God was asking me not to bind up my heart but to leave it open, to have a broken and open heart so God's love could flow from my heart to the world. So I began to pray, *"O Lord, make my heart broken and open."*

That prayer, however, didn't take away all the pain. I've discovered prayer isn't like an aspirin tablet that we take and, poof, a half hour later the pain is gone. Prayer is more like a microscope that reveals more and more of what is unseen to the human eye.

Unpeeling the Layers

I kept praying and asking the Lord to reveal to me the source of my pain, and this is what he showed me:

Loss of a Love

The first layer, of course, was the loss of a love. It was difficult and painful to let a romance die. But there was more.

Loss of Hope

The second layer was the loss of hope. Like most women, I was guilty of having the future all planned out: We were going to spend Thanksgiving and Christmas together. I was planning to surprise him for his birthday, and I was even thinking of moving closer to him so we could spend more time together.

Now, suddenly, I was forced to reimage my future without him, and it seemed impossible. Who would I go inline skating, sailing, and dancing with? Who would hold me and kiss me and bring sunshine and laughter into my life? Who would help carry the burden of my life? I was struggling with a major loss of hope.

But the Lord didn't leave me in this state for long. In fact, the day after I realized I was suffering from a major loss of hope, a woman from Canada called and asked me to lead a retreat for 200 women the following year. Just when I felt as if the lens of my world was closing, the Lord was opening it up. He was using a wide-angle lens to help me see new possibilities and new opportunities for the future without this romance.

Slumbering Giant

Finally, the third layer penetrated closer to the heart of the matter. All my desires for intimacy, companionship, and even marriage resurfaced. My romantic passions had been reawakened within me like a slumbering giant, and had nowhere to go.

That's what hurt so much. This man had waltzed—well, he'd tangoed—into my life, stirred up my desires for intimacy and romance, and then left. And I was powerless to do anything. I was powerless to change him, powerless to make him love me, powerless to make someone else love me. With this understanding the last layer peeled off, and I was left staring at the core of my pain: my deep need to belong.

Wanting to Belong

I thought I would belong to this man. I thought I would belong to his world, to the future we would build together, to the life we would share dancing, teaching tango, and raising a family. This was the deepest source of my pain—feeling as if I had nowhere to belong.

With this realization, God began a new work in me. He showed me I did belong to someone. I belong to Christ. I began telling myself a dozen times a day, "I belong to Christ. I belong to Christ." Sitting at my computer, driving the car, washing dishes, I kept repeating over and over, "I belong to Christ."

Not only that, I also realized I belong to the body of Christ. I belong to my dear friend Maureen in San Diego, to Donna in Buffalo, to Jane in Louisiana, to C. C. in New York. I belong to my son, Michael, to the kids I teach in my confirmation class, to the women in my faith sharing group. I even belong to you. This was the beginning of living not just as a daughter, but as a bride.

A Wider View of Love

When most people think of spousal love, they restrict it to the love between husband and wife. God, however, wants to open the lens of our minds and give us a wider view. He's inviting each of us not only to be a daughter of the Father, but to be a bride, the bride of the Spirit. He's inviting you into spousal union with himself.

Now you may be thinking, "Time out! I can handle being a daughter of the Father, but living in spousal union with God? You've got to be kidding! Isn't that just for saints and ultraholy people?"

Yes, it is for saints and holy people, but we're all called to holiness, we're all called to be saints. You can't check an "exempt" box on the form of life to opt out. Living in spousal union with God is for all of us.

If this shocks you, I understand. Sometimes it takes a while for new and unfamiliar ideas to gain entrance to the castle of our minds. We see this pattern even in the Gospels.

At the Last Supper, Jesus bends to wash Peter's feet. Immediately, Peter puts up a fight. The idea of the Teacher washing his disciples' feet is just too shocking. It makes Peter's brain lock up. But Jesus doesn't give up. He gently explains the purpose of his actions, and Peter jumps on board, begging for an entire bath!

If you're feeling a bit like Peter and your brain is locking up, give it a rest. Let a spousal relationship with God remain on the other side of the moat for a while. When it doesn't seem so strange, let the drawbridge of your heart down, relax, and pick up this book again.

A Divine Date?

If you're only mildly in shock, you're probably wondering, "How do we enter into spousal union with God?" Do we e-mail him to make a date?

Let me share something that's a mystery to me: *The only way we enter into spousal union with God is through pain and suffering.* I know it sounds crazy, but that seems to be the way it works. And it works this way because God has to create in us more room for himself.

Most of us live with lots of interior clutter. We have attachments, guilt, anger, and fear that take up interior space and crowd out God. It's kind of like spiritual cholesterol—the clutter clogs our interior life and reduces the flow of grace within us.

So what does God do? He undertakes some serious interior housecleaning to remove the interior clutter. But that's painful. It's painful to let go of the things we depend on for security, that give us pats on the back, that allow us to think we're in control.

In case you hadn't noticed, women have a huge need for

security. As a result, we cling to things and people. We cling to our hopes for the future. We even cling to old wounds and patterns because they're familiar.

God knows this. He also knows that in order to espouse us to himself, he has to create in us more room for himself. He has to hollow us out.

This was the marvelous work I realized God was doing in me. Through the pain and loss, he was carving in me more room for himself. He was making a bridal chamber where only he could dwell.

Heartache

How did I know this? Instead of ignoring the pain in my heart or trying to rise above it, I began using the pain as a constant invitation to conversation with God. As I was working, folding laundry, or drifting off to sleep, I allowed the constant ache in my heart to remind me to talk to God, to pray.

As I did this, slowly the pain began to feel different. Instead of a gaping hole through which all my insides spilled out, the wound began to have a warmth, a presence. It became a divine wound that sparkled in my soul constantly reminding me of God's presence. I understood that God was espousing me to himself. He was making me his bride, and this was a diamond in my soul that was his betrothal ring to me.

More Intimacy

The thing that intrigues me about this whole experience is that I had nothing to do with it. If it had been up to me, I would have been married to my tango friend and dancing happily ever after. But that wasn't God's intention. Instead, he wanted to reawaken in me a desire for spousal love on the human level in order to create in me a deeper capacity for spousal love on the divine level.

Forgive me if I repeat that sentence: *God wanted to reawaken in me a desire for spousal love on the human level in order to create in me a deeper capacity for spousal love on the divine level.*

He wasn't allowing pain and suffering in my life just for the sake of pain and suffering. It had a purpose. My ache for human intimacy opened the drawbridge of my heart to the possibility of divine intimacy.

Shortly after this experience, I tried to capture the sovereignty of God's action through poetry:

Diamond, diamond in my soul.
How did you get there?
If it was me,
I would not know.

But it is You, You are the Jeweler
Who wounds with a gem of love.
You make the mark so deep,
Chiseled there by pain.

How can a wound be one of love?
How can pain be that of deepening?

For You did not wait for my consent,
Nor hesitate, pending my approval.
The setting is ready; the diamond awaits.
The circumstances conspire their approval.

Now the breaking happens.
My heart is broken and open.

No mending, no binding,
Just broken and open for love.

You place the jewel within,
Its light flashing through the fog of my pain;
A constant reminder of your promise to me.
A constant reminder of your presence.

The diamond, the promise,
They find no origin in me.
They are symbols of your extravagant love,
A covenant wrought solely by the Jeweler's hand.

Ordinary Spousal Living

In response to this divine wound of love, I began telling the Lord that I wished I could live as the spouse of the Spirit. Quite to my surprise, he showed me that I already was. I was thinking of spiritual espousal as some future reality, as something to do with mystical ecstasy. This may be true for some, but living as the spouse of the Spirit is much more concrete than that. It's living our daily lives in union with God.

When someone gets married, that person is bonded to the other person and carries a sense of that bond wherever he or she goes, whether it's to work, shopping, or golf.

The same is true of a spousal relationship with God. He goes with us wherever we go. It's impossible to separate who we are from our relationship with God. Even though we may not express our faith explicitly in everything we do, just as married people don't talk about their spouse in every conversation, still our faith is inseparable from who we are and what we do.

We flip pancakes in union with God. We ride the subway in union with God. We take out the trash in union with God.

So please, even though it hurts, don't be afraid of the pain. It's the Divine Artist's tool to carve in you more room for himself, to prepare the bridal chamber.

Secondly, it's worth repeating that a spousal life isn't just for a select group of mystics and saints. Neither is it a communion of spirits that happens only when you get all your kids down for a nap at the same time, or lock yourself in the bathroom for ten glorious minutes, or retire from work or mothering and enter the convent. It's a grace available in the here and now for everyone.

John Paul II repeatedly called for a new springtime and a new evangelization. The prophet Isaiah says of God, "I am about to do a new thing; now it springs forth, do you not perceive it?" (Is 43:19).

God is doing something new. Never in the Church's history has God offered this bridal invitation in such a lavish manner to laity and religious alike. It's part of God's new springtime. It's our bridal boot camp for the new evangelization.

What a funny phrase—bridal boot camp! (Doesn't it make you think of a bunch of soldiers running through an obstacle course in wedding gowns?) However, like military boot camp, God uses pain and suffering in our lives to condition us for the task ahead, to bring about greater detachment from our way of doing things and a greater freedom to respond to his invitations.

The new evangelization isn't a "same-old, same-old" presentation of the Gospel. It's lay people like you and me entering into a bridal relationship with God himself. That's new. That will rock the world!

A Spousal God

Besides the abundant availability of this spousal grace, there's another reason why a spousal life is for all of us: because God is spousal.

God is not just one person. God is a Trinity of persons: a union and communion of fruitful, self-giving love among the Father, Son, and Holy Spirit. God in his very being is spousal. That means that whenever God acts, it's always for the purpose of union.

If you take only one thought away from this book, let it be this: *God always acts for the purpose of union.* Put it over your sink. Tape it to the inside of the dryer door. Post it on your steering wheel. God always acts for the purpose of union.

If today you're diagnosed with breast cancer or your teenage son is arrested, God is acting for the purpose of union. If next week, your financial debt surpasses the height of Mount Everest or you want to strangle your boss (or husband), God is acting for the purpose of union. If you feel you can't wake up one more day alone or depressed, God is acting for the purpose of union.

In the Old Testament, God constantly wooed Israel back to himself through tragedy, famine, and trial. He always acted for the purpose of union.

In the New Testament, Saint Paul transposes this nuptial imagery to an entirely new level. In Ephesians 5, he writes: "For this reason a man will leave his father and mother and be joined to his wife, and the two will become one flesh. This is a great mystery, and I am applying it to Christ and the church" (Eph 5:31–32).

Marriage: The Great Mystery

I pondered this Scripture for years until finally it hit me: marriage is a "sneak preview" of the spousal union God wants to have with us. The great mystery is not only that husband and wife become one flesh, but also that we can become one with God in a way that surpasses marital union. We can become the spouse of the Spirit.

Listen to God's tender words spoken through the prophet Hosea: "I will take you for my wife forever; I will take you for my wife in righteousness and in justice, in steadfast love, and in mercy. I will take you for my wife in faithfulness; and you shall know the LORD" (2:19–20).

The great mystery is that God wants to marry us! We not only have a universal vocation, a feminine vocation, and a unique vocation, we also have a final vocation, a vocation in heaven. Every woman's journey finds its consummation in this vocation. John Paul II speaks about this final (or eschatological) vocation when he reflects on Jesus' conversation with the Sadducees.

One Bride for Seven Brothers?

The Sadducees contrive a ridiculous scenario in which a woman successively marries seven brothers. Each one dies without leaving any children. They ask Jesus: Whose wife will she will be in the resurrection of the dead? The Sadducees are sure Jesus will either deny the resurrection of the dead or endorse a type of heavenly polygamy. Instead, Jesus chooses a third alternative. He responds: "Is not this the reason you are wrong, that you know neither the scriptures nor the power of God? For when they rise from the dead, they neither marry nor are given in marriage, but are like angels in heaven" (Mk 12:24–25).

Married to God!

In heaven, we neither marry nor are given in marriage because we are espoused to God himself! The spousal meaning of the body finds its ultimate fulfillment through spousal union with God in heaven. This is the reason we were created and saved—not just to be "safe" from the fires of hell, but to be spousally united with God forever.

Revelation, the last book of the Bible, ends with the marriage celebration of Christ and the Church (19:7, 21:2, 9–10). This is the fulfillment of time and history. Time and history exist to reunite Christ and his bride.

The bride of Christ, however, is not just a biblical manner of speaking. We are the bride. We are the Church. Each of us enters the jubilee door of heaven as a bride adorned for her wedding.

Doubly Spousal

For those who have the privilege of already being a bride here on earth, this invitation to a spousal relationship with God may seem confusing. It almost feels as if I'm asking you to be married to two spouses or to minimize your relationship with your husband in favor of a spousal relationship with God. Be assured I am not suggesting either.

God designed human marriage to be a reflection of our heavenly marriage with God, not a fierce competitor with it. This is why the Catholic Church considers marriage a sacrament, a particular way that God reveals himself on earth and conveys his love to us. In other words, marriage as a sacrament is a visible sign of an invisible reality. Through marriage, we can glimpse the invisible reality of heaven; we can "see" our eternal vocation, which is to be spousally united to Christ forever. In God's master plan, human marriage makes visible the *eternal* spousal meaning of the body.

In Ephesians 5, Saint Paul also speaks of the husband's role to love his wife as Christ loved the Church. In other words, a husband is to be "Christ" to his bride (more about this in chapter 7). When a married woman loves her husband, when she encourages, respects, and honors him, she is, in truth, loving Christ in a particular way. Her allegiances are not divided, but united within marriage—she loves Christ directly and she loves the image of Christ within her spouse. Both these realities are meant to increase a married woman's capacity for spousal union.

What was true of my tango relationship is even more profoundly true of the marital relationship: God wants to increase your capacity for spousal love on the human level in order to increase your capacity for spousal love on the divine level. Those who are married get direct, concrete practice at growing in spousal love every day, right in their own homes, kitchens, and bedrooms.

Heaven on Earth

Fortunately, none of us, whether single or married, has to wait until heaven to experience our final vocation. Christ, our Bridegroom, has already given us his body and blood. He made a total, complete, and irrevocable gift of himself to us upon the cross. And he's left his total, complete, and irrevocable gift of himself to us in the Eucharist.

The Eucharist, as Scott Hahn loves to say, is our heaven on earth.[1] It's where time and eternity meet. When we receive Jesus' body and blood, we enter into one-flesh union with him. In those precious moments of eucharistic communion, bride and Bridegroom are so united as to be one flesh. We leave father, mother, spouse, and children to cling to our Bridegroom and become one body with him.

Banquet Table or Bridal Chamber?

This is not the language of symbol; it's the language of reality. If the Eucharist were only a symbol, Jesus would be inviting us to the banquet table, to come and sit next to him. But it's more than a symbol. The Eucharist *is* the body and blood of Christ. Jesus invites us to the bridal chamber, to one-flesh union with himself.

Jesus insists in John 6 that he is speaking literally, not figuratively, about his body and blood. When the crowds question his literal language, he doesn't say, "Oh, no, you misunderstood me," as he did in other instances, for example, with Nicodemus (Jn 3), the woman at the well (Jn 4), and Lazarus' sister Martha (Jn 11). Instead, he reaffirms with even more authority: "Very truly, I tell you, unless you eat the flesh of the Son of Man and drink his blood, you have no life in you.... Those who eat my flesh and drink my blood abide in me, and I in them" (Jn 6:53, 56).

Jesus Completes His Mission

Jesus couldn't have backed down. It would have betrayed his whole mission. The human race would remain unwed. The Father's plan from all eternity to enter into spousal union with us would remain unfinished.

Instead, on the cross Jesus declared, "It is finished." God's plan for mankind was consummated. Christopher West, an author and speaker on John Paul II's theology of the body, describes Jesus' gift of self this way: "Christ left his Father in heaven. He left the home of his Mother on earth—to give up his body for his Bride, so that we might become 'one flesh' with him."[2]

The Greatest Gift

The Real Presence of Jesus in the Eucharist is the greatest gift God has ever given to mankind. It is the gift of his very self to us. In the Eucharist, God gives himself to us not only spiritually, but physically as well.

This reveals the most profound truth about the human body. *The body is not only spousal, but eucharistic.* It's made for spousal union between husband and wife *and* for one-flesh union between each person and Christ.

Communion, Not Contraception

We shouldn't be surprised that as belief in and devotion to the Real Presence declines, sexual activity outside of marriage skyrockets. The two are related. The deepest yearning in our hearts is for spousal union.

Consequently, when we fail to experience the Eucharist as spousal union with Christ, we search for this union elsewhere. Instead of teaching our young people the finer points of contraceptive use, we should teach them how to live the eucharistic life.

The eucharistic life is the antidote to the sexual revolution. It reverses the "maximum pleasure / minimum effort" trend of the past forty years and returns us to a Love that suffers, a Love that lays down its life for another, a Love that is total, faithful, fruitful, and irrevocable.

Prolonging the Real Presence in the World

Igniting a eucharistic revolution doesn't mean every person has to join a cloister and spend the rest of his or her life in perpetual adoration. Rather, it means the union and communion we experience in the Eucharist become the reality out of which we live every moment of the day. Whether we're at work, home, or the football stadium, our words and actions should prolong Christ's Real Presence in the world. As single, married, or celibate Christians, our lives should be ones of fruitful, self-giving love.

Twelve Ways to Live the Spousal Life

Perhaps this sounds a bit abstract, so let's get concrete. How do we practically live this moment-by-moment union with God? How can we jump into the spousal current on the fourth part of the journey? Here are twelve suggestions drawn from my own life. Please don't feel you have to implement them all at once. Let the Holy Spirit show you how to begin and how to proceed.

1. Be More—Do Less

So often we think we have to "do" more. The last thing I want to do is pile more on your already full plate. One of my hopes for this book has been to help you "be" more: Be more as a daughter of God; be more as a woman; be more as the unique person God created you to be. As you live more deeply out of your being, I think you will find that you are driven to do less. After all, we're human *beings*, not human *doings*. You don't *do* a bride; you *are* a bride.

2. Discover "Prayer of the Moment"

Spend time with your Divine Spouse; this is what we call prayer. Many people complain they don't have time to pray, so I'd like to share with you the secret of spousal prayer. It's called "prayer of the moment": whatever is going on in the moment, I use to prompt me to pray.

When I'm washing dishes, I pray: "Thank you, Jesus, that you wash away our sins." When I'm folding laundry, I pray: "Lord, please fold me (or whoever's clothes I'm folding) in your love and mercy." When I open the door to walk out, I pray: "Jesus, help me to open the door of my heart to you." When I turn the key in the lock, I pray: "Jesus, help me never to lock the door of my heart to you."

When I introduced this idea to a confirmation class I was teaching, they really got into the spirit. Here are some of the prayers of the moment they came up with: Feeling the sun: "Lord, help me feel the warmth of your look." Carrying a book bag: "Jesus, thank you that you carry my burdens." Chewing bubble gum: "Lord, may I chew on your word." Driving in the car: "Jesus, lead me in the right path." Doing math: "Help me to forgive others seventy times seven times."

I especially love three things about prayer of the moment:

✧ We can never say we're too busy because it doesn't take extra time—it just takes being present to the moment.

✧ We can teach our children how to pray this way, so that prayer becomes part of their culture from an early age.

✧ It changes the way we react to circumstances in our lives. Instead of cursing a red light, we can pray, "Thank you, Jesus, that I will never be late to heaven." Instead of getting angry over spilled milk, we can say, "Thank you, Jesus, that you fill our cup to overflowing." We can use the circumstances around us to constantly bring us into union with God.

3. Get Your Senses Involved

Rediscover the rich visual treasures of the Christian faith. Sacred art, statues, Advent wreaths, Stations of the Cross, different images of Our Lady, the Divine Mercy image, and

Scripture verses placed around the house are visual ways to redirect our focus to God. Before I sit down at my computer to work, I sometimes light a candle and ask the Lord to guide my work. The candle is a warm reminder of the Lord's presence beside me.

Maybe you could light a candle in the kitchen while washing dishes, or in the living room while you're cleaning house, or wherever you might be. Then, every time you see the candle, allow it to bring you back into God's presence. (But please don't leave it unattended or forget to blow it out!)

4. Get Your Hearing Involved

Put a small CD or MP3 player in whatever room you're in the most (make sure you have one in the car), and then use it. Play talks on spiritual subjects,[3] listen to the Bible, and play Christian music. Sometimes we need something outside of us to stimulate our minds and nourish our thoughts about our Divine Spouse.

Often women complain that their minds get flabby because they haven't had an adult conversation in weeks, or they're overwhelmed by multiple domestic tasks, or they spend hours a day chauffeuring kids in the car or caring for an elderly parent. Use the time when your hands are busy but your mind is free to stimulate your thoughts about different aspects of the faith, listen to Scripture, and lead your spirit into worship.

5. Read the Lives of the Saints

If you don't have time to read the lives of the saints by yourself, then read to your children, no matter how old they are. The most valuable present I received at Michael's birth was a series of simple books about the saints. That's how I began learning about the saints. Then, as my son grew, our stories became more sophisticated. You can read about the saints at the dinner table, bedtime, or family time. If you don't have children, read the biographies and writings of the saints and let them show you how to live a spousal life.

6. Celebrate the Lord's Day

Sunday is the wedding day of our soul. God doesn't celebrate his wedding anniversary to us once a year, but every week. Every Sunday we're reminded that we are made for union and communion with God. When we rest from our work, it allows the spousal meaning of the body to resurrect.

This means letting go of the things we want to *do* so we can *be* more: Invite others over for Sunday brunch (but make it simple so you don't end up cooking, doing dishes, and cleaning up instead of enjoying your family and friends); play soccer, go to the beach, or build snowmen as a family. If you're single, you could volunteer for Big Brothers or Big Sisters, spend time in eucharistic adoration, call a friend long-distance, go bike riding, or have dinner with a family.

Except for rare occasions, I avoid doing laundry and housework on Sunday, and I try not to mow the lawn or go grocery shopping. I require my son to do his homework on Friday or Saturday and not wait until Sunday. This way it's really a day for him, God, and our friends. It takes discipline and planning to set aside the Lord's Day every week, but it's an invaluable way to nourish a spousal rhythm of life. (If you would like some extra inspiration on this topic, John Paul II's apostolic letter, *Dies Domini: On Keeping the Lord's Day Holy*, is a great reminder of the meaning and purpose of Sunday.)

7. Make Time for Feminine Fellowship

Get together with other women to pray, laugh, cry, and blow off steam. As women, we need to develop close relationships with other women, to share our being with them, and to remind one another who we are in all our feminine fullness and originality. Meet with a small group of women two or three times a month, or commit yourself to calling someone on the phone once a week to keep in regular contact.

Ask your pastor about organizing a women's prayer breakfast, Lenten morning of reflection, or day of retreat. Remember, you don't just belong to Christ. You belong to the body of Christ.

8. Read John Paul II's Writings

Start with John Paul II's *Letter to Women* and his *Letter to Families*. Then read *On the Dignity and Vocation of Women* (*Mulieris Dignitatem*). After that, consider reading *The Gospel of Life* (*Evangelium Vitae*), *The Role of the Christian Family in the Modern World* (*Familiaris Consortio*), or *The Lay Members of Christ's Faithful People* (*Christifideles Laici*). [4]

One of my goals has been to give you a primer in John Paul II's thought, a glimpse at his "ABCs." Now, when you read his writings, either on your own or in a group, I hope you'll understand what he means by sincere gift of self, spousal meaning of the body, and motherhood according to the Spirit. Then, allow the Holy Spirit to weave these concepts into your life and your vocabulary.

9. Ask God to Make You a Saint

My favorite theologian, Father Francis Martin, says a saint is someone in whom God works out the problem of the age. The problem of our age is precisely what we've been reflecting on in this book: what it means to be male and female.

Many Christian women are afraid of radical feminism because it redefines the human person and gender. Feminism, however, is pushing the Church forward in articulating her understanding of masculinity, femininity, and the body. Perhaps the Lord wants you to be part of this exciting development of doctrine. Give the Lord permission to work out in your life the problem of the age and let the Holy Spirit show you what it means to be daughter, woman, and bride in the context of your unique life.

10. Teach Your Sons How to Live a Spousal Life

Have you noticed how much easier it is for girls to be spiritual than boys? I saw this clearly when I was doing an hour of eucharistic adoration and my neighbor brought her two girls, ages eight and ten. They sweetly prayed for forty-five minutes when my son (who was eleven) wouldn't have lasted ten! We're doing a great job raising our girls to be godly women, but I ask you, whom are they going to marry?

This really concerns me. We need to teach our sons, grandsons, nephews, and godsons to live for union and communion through a sincere gift of self, not just for earning a living or being a professional basketball player. (More about this topic in chapter 7.)

11. Cultivate the Eucharistic Life

Try to come into contact with the Real Presence of Jesus in the Eucharist more often. If you go to Mass once a week, try going twice. If you spend an hour in eucharistic adoration once a week, stop in for ten or fifteen minutes another time during the week. If there's no adoration chapel near you, pray before the tabernacle on your way to work or while the children are in school.

Matthew Kelly, an international speaker born in Australia, says his time before the Blessed Sacrament is when he lets things float to the top of his heart, where he skims off what doesn't need to be there. That's a good model for all of us. Don't worry about what you're going to say. Just show up and let Jesus skim off from your heart and life what doesn't need to be there.

The key to growing in eucharistic life is sustainability. Figure out what you can do over the long haul and then be faithful to it. And most of all, receive the Eucharist fervently, realizing that the great mystery is taking place in you as you receive the Body and Blood of Christ. In this moment, you and God are one. Don't rush your eucharistic communion. Extend your thanksgiving as long as possible. Remember, this is a foretaste of eternal life.

12. Cultivate Your Relationship with Mary

The Blessed Mother is such a gift to us! Mary is the most perfect human example of the spousal life. She was the first to fully live the great mystery, to live a bridal relationship with the Trinity. This is why she is called the Spouse of the Spirit.

God's Rainbow

Over the years, the Catholic Church's emphasis on Mary has been vigorously criticized. Isn't Jesus enough? Why do we need Mary? Doesn't she detract from Jesus' saving death?

Far from detracting from Jesus' life and death, Mary is the rainbow of God. Mary, like a rainbow, makes it possible to see what's usually hidden from view. Even though we know light is composed of a spectrum of colors, we see the fullness of this truth when a beautiful rainbow arches across the sky.

Likewise, even though we know Jesus' death upon the cross forgives sin and heals our relationship with God, we see the fullness of this truth when we gaze upon the beauty of Mary arching across history.

Everything the Church says about Mary flows from the cross and God's generosity. God paints the rainbow of Mary to make the abstract truths of the faith concrete for *us*.

Mary's Greatest Need

One Good Friday, I was preparing to venerate the cross when a new thought struck me: As Mary stood at the foot of the cross, she not only shed tears of sorrow, but also tears of gratitude. She was witnessing *her* salvation. *Mary wasn't the one least in need of the cross. She was the one most in need of the cross* [5] because God applied the redemption of the cross to her *in advance.*

Saved from the Pit...in Advance

If the idea of receiving the grace of the cross in advance seems odd, perhaps this image will help: Imagine you are walking along a road and suddenly you fall into a deep pit. Can you get out by yourself? No, you're condemned to die. But then someone comes along and pulls you out of the pit. Are you saved? Absolutely yes.

Now imagine you're walking along that same road and the person comes to take you down a different path so you don't fall into the pit. Are you saved from the pit? Absolutely yes, but *in advance*.

This is the grace of the Immaculate Conception. Mary was saved from the pit of sin in advance through the cross of Christ. She received the grace of living in union with God, others, nature, and within herself, between her body and spirit, from the moment of her conception. Her ability to live in union and communion was fully intact.

Immaculate Duct Tape

When I try to explain this idea to audiences, I often bring with me a piece of duct tape. A fresh piece of duct tape has its ability for union fully intact. If I stick it to something, it sticks and sticks well. But if I peel it off and stick it to something else, it sticks, but not as well. If I do that a dozen times, by the end, the duct tapes barely adheres. Its ability for union is compromised.

Because of sin in our lives, most of us are like that piece of duct tape. We stick ourselves to something or someone, peel ourselves off, stick ourselves somewhere else, and so on. In the process, our ability for union becomes compromised. (Thank goodness for the sacrament of Reconciliation, which restores our ability for union.)

In using the language of mortal sin, the Church is not label-ing the sinner as bad. Instead, the Church is clearly reminding us that the sin is so serious that the sinner loses the ability for union through his or her consciously chosen action. As a result, it's impossible to "stick" to God until the person repents.

Mary, on the other hand, is like immaculate duct tape. She adheres once and only once. Through her own free will coop-erating with God's grace, she preserved the purity of her abil-ity for union and communion. She never sinned or broke her union with God. She always made a sincere gift of herself to God first of all, and to others out of love for God.

Making the Trinity Concrete

Mary is a precious gift to each Christian because Mary is an icon of the Trinity. In her, the entire mystery of the Trinity is enfleshed: The Holy Spirit espouses himself to Mary to con-ceive the Word of God in her and lead all creation back to the Father. Mary is daughter of the Father, mother of the Savior, and bride of the Spirit.

As we say yes, we become more like Mary. We enter more deeply into the self-giving mystery of the Trinity, and the Holy Spirit helps to heal the spousal meaning of our body. Through our daily life in the Spirit, we gradually recover our ability to live in union and communion with God, with others, with nature, and within ourselves, between body and spirit.

The Marian Way

As Christian women, we don't have to wonder where the current is taking us. Mary has illuminated the path before us:

⤞ The Holy Spirit wants to espouse us to himself to conceive the Word of God in us and lead all creation back to the Father.

⤞ Each of us is a daughter of the Father, spiritual mother of the Savior, and spouse of the Spirit.

⤞ We are created to image God in our feminine bodies, to bear Christ to the world, and to live in moment-by-moment union with our Divine Bridegroom even in the midst of pain and busyness.

Eucharistic, Trinitarian, Bridal, and Marian

Whether we are single, married, or celibate, our feminine journey is truly eucharistic, Trinitarian, bridal, and Marian. No wonder John Paul II believed that in Mary we discover the true genius of woman and that this discovery must reach the heart of every woman and shape her vocation and life.[6]

May the third millennium find the imprint of Mary on every woman's heart to help us fall in love with our feminine genius. Mary, Mother of the Third Millennium, pray for us!

QUESTIONS FOR REFLECTION AND DISCUSSION

1. Have you ever thought of yourself as the spouse of the Spirit?

2. What type of interior clutter takes up space within you and prevents you from making more room for God? Are you willing to give God permission to clean house?

3. What is your reaction to the statement: "God always acts for the purpose of union"? What experiences in your life confirm or challenge this belief?

4. Review the twelve suggestions for living a spousal life. Which of them are you already living? Which ones could you integrate into your life?

5. How do you pray now? Could prayer of the moment help enrich your relationship with your Divine Spouse? Compose three prayers of the moment based on activities you do every day.

6. Why is Mary so important to the life of the Church? How would you describe your relationship with Mary?

7. Write a prayer to Jesus telling him your thoughts and feelings about being his bride.

CHAPTER 7

What About the Men?

A FUNNY THING HAPPENS after I speak about the dignity and vocation of women. I'm often surrounded by women anxiously asking: "What about the men?" I kept hoping John Paul II would let me off the hook by publishing an apostolic letter specifically on the dignity and vocation of men, but he didn't. [1]

As a result of those questions, I've continued to pray, read John Paul II's writings, and talk to men about their life experiences. I've also pondered the distinctive structure of the masculine body to try to understand what it reveals about the masculine gift of self. Just as women have an empty space within that reveals their unique call to spiritual motherhood, so too, I mused, there must be a male counterpart that arises from the masculine physiology. The seemingly obvious counterpart would be spiritual fatherhood, and yet I felt dissatisfied with this conclusion. It didn't seem to capture the unique element of the masculine body. I felt there had to be something more. And while it took two years of prayer and reflection for the answer to surface, I can assure you, it was worth the wait! I hope you will agree.

What follows are my original reflections on the masculine gift of self. These thoughts are not intended to present a doctrinal teaching of the Catholic Church, but are my attempt to spur men to reflect more deeply on their nature as men and encourage them to develop these ideas even further. I also hope women will gain more patience and appreciation for the uniqueness of men and why God purposefully created us male and female.

Back to the Beginning (Again!)

To understand the nature of men, we once again follow John Paul II back to the beginning, back to creation and the Fall in Genesis, chapters 2 and 3.

As I mentioned in chapter 2, John Paul II identified a deep and original unity between male and female. Women and men are not from different planets. They're from the same body. We are one nature, embodied in two ways, for the purpose of union and communion through a sincere gift of self.

This is what John Paul II called the spousal meaning of the body, and it's the bottom line for understanding both masculine and feminine nature. (Forgive me for repeating myself. It's something I learned from John Paul II.)

In chapter 3, we saw woman's first presence in the world was as gift to man. But now let's turn the scenario around and look at it from the male's perspective (with a little help from John Paul II).

Receiver of the Gift

If woman's first presence in the world is as gift, then man is the one who, above all, receives the gift: "The woman has 'from the beginning' been entrusted to his eyes, to his consciousness, to his sensibility, to his 'heart.' "[2]

This is a beautiful image. Adam spontaneously opened his heart and life to Eve without hesitation or limitation. He didn't complain to God that she wasn't just like him, nor did he simply tolerate her presence. He accepted and loved her with all her feminine distinctiveness and uniqueness.[3]

Through accepting fully the gift of woman, man discovered the spousal meaning of his own body. He discovered that he, too, was made for a sincere gift of self, for a communion of persons and not just a solitary existence. John Paul II says it is the *man's* responsibility to protect this mutual self-giving because it is through *reciprocal* self-giving that a real communion of persons is formed.[4]

Gift Versus Appropriation

However, something happened to this communion of persons. It didn't stay reciprocal for long because Satan entered the picture. One of the most important concepts Genesis teaches is this: When God acts, he gifts. When Satan acts, he appropriates. He takes for his own purposes.

This is graphically dramatized in the garden. When God acted, he made all creation as a gift of his love. When Satan acted, he convinced Eve to take and appropriate the fruit for self-gain instead of self-giving.[5]

Where Was Adam?

But Eve is not the only one involved in original sin. There's an important and sometimes forgotten question that must be asked: Where was Adam? He must have been close by because Eve gave him the fruit to eat.

Yet Adam's silence is deafening. He failed to intervene on Eve's behalf, to protect the communion of persons entrusted to him. He opted for mute passivity rather than self-donation. The original communion of persons shared by Adam and Eve with each other and God was shattered.

Adam's failure to protect the original communion of persons is worth pondering. Dr. Larry Crabb, a Christian psychologist in the United States, has written an excellent book called *The Silence of Adam* in which he looks at why men fail to act.[6]

He says most men draw their worth and identity from feeling competent. Therefore, they live within the boundaries of their competency, investing time and energy in goals and achievements where they feel capable. This makes them feel like men.

Life, however, is not always so neat or predictable. Men are confronted by unfamiliar territory—by situations where their adequacy may be questioned, their talents appear useless, or their best efforts can't control the outcome.

When this happens, a sinister voice creeps in. It accuses them of being incompetent and unmanly. In response, men often become paralyzed by fear and retreat into passivity or they try to dominate the situation. In the story of original sin, we see both happening.

Sound the Retreat!

Adam first slips into passivity—he fails to intervene on Eve's behalf. He chooses to be silent rather than confront the relational chaos Satan is brewing.

Dr. Crabb says this pattern is repeated over and over again. Men retreat into their work, hobbies, or sports rather than entering into the relational sphere. They withdraw their gift of self from woman, leaving her to do the initiating and sometimes even the protecting.

The Fear Factor

Men do this out of fear—fear of entering the realm of mystery where the path before them is uncharted and they have to live in the unresolved. Every man I've ever spoken to tells me he hates to live in the unresolved. It's too messy. Most men dread watching another person (especially a woman) experience pain and suffering, particularly if a man feels helpless to do anything about it.

A Crying Woman

In our home, I'm always looking for opportunities to teach my son how to relate to women. One day, I plopped on the bed next to him and asked, "Michael, what do you do when a woman cries?"

He looked at me as if I'd finally gone off my rocker. Then he thought for a moment and said, "Hold her?"

"Yes! Yes!" I exulted, and gave him a big feminine hug.

Why do I torture my son with questions like this? Because when a man feels helpless, his basic instinct is to run and hide, to withdraw his gift of self because he doesn't think receiving and protecting a woman's gift of self is enough. (It is enough!)

Independent Women/Absent Men

The outcome is resentful women and absent men. Women stop giving their gift of self to men and become independent women who don't need men, and men become confused about their identity because their competency is no longer valued or needed.

In short, when men fail to act, women develop an independency that excludes a real communion of persons. The result is isolation.

Domination Replaces Self-Donation

Original sin has a second unfortunate consequence, which is domination ("he shall rule over you"). Original sin takes the communion of persons and twists it a different way. Instead of self-donation, domination triumphs. It tempts men to regard a woman as a something instead of a someone.

In essence, domination reduces a woman from a person to an object. It zeroes in on the physical dimension and ignores the spiritual reality. A woman's body, and a man's as well, are no longer valued because they are made in the image and likeness of God for a sincere gift of self, but because they provide the means for gratification, pleasure, and release, whether through intercourse, pornography, self-stimulation, or physical or emotional abuse.

Disposable Bodies

Unfortunately, Satan has done a masterful job of using our desires and passions to destroy the real communion of persons and the divine significance of the body. In the garden, woman revealed to man the meaning of his existence: to exist with and for another, to make a sincere gift of self for *permanent* union and communion.

With original sin and the introduction of domination, the body is no longer treated as a gift but as a consumer object. It can be appropriated and enjoyed for the moment and then disposed of without thinking of its divine image or value.

After original sin, the pendulum swings two ways: man finds himself retreating from woman and the result is silence and isolation, or he appropriates woman and the result is power and domination.

The Third Way

Obviously there must be a third way, and this was the one I had been diligently pondering. The answer came to me in November 1998 when I was 31,000 feet in the air and had nowhere to go.

I was flying back to the United States after speaking in Trinidad, West Indies, and I was enjoying the tranquil turquoise blue water of the Bahamas below. I was also reading *They Called Her the Baroness*,[7] a biography of Catherine de Hueck Doherty, founder of Madonna House in Ontario, Canada.

Catherine and her husband, Eddie, married later in life. Eventually, they decided to live a celibate marriage as a sign of solidarity with the single people who shared their ministry. As a result, Eddie felt called to the ordained priesthood, and he petitioned the Holy See twice for permission to become a priest. Twice he was denied.

One day a priest friend from the Melkite Rite, an Eastern Catholic rite with married priests, visited Catherine and Eddie. Eddie shared his struggle about priesthood. Their friend offhandedly replied that if he was ever consecrated a bishop, he would ordain Eddie a priest. A week later, their friend was chosen to be a bishop.

At that moment, something broke inside me and I began to cry. I was surprised at my reaction because I identify more with Catherine than Eddie. Like me, Catherine was a writer, speaker, and single mother for many years. Why would I be so moved that her seventy-eight-year-old husband received permission to be ordained a priest?

I composed myself and continued reading. Three paragraphs later, tears poured down my face. Eddie had returned to Madonna House after his ordination, and Catherine's first words to him were, "Your blessing, Father." *Eddie was no longer simply husband to Catherine, but priest.*

This was the answer I had been seeking for two years: that the nature of the male is not passivity or power but priestly.

Why is this the nature of the male?

This question takes us right back to the masculine body. The male body is distinctively external. It is made to penetrate, to go out of itself. It is made to literally give its body and blood—its semen—away.

There is a profound connection between this distinctively masculine truth and the priesthood. In the Old Testament, only the priest was allowed to offer the body and blood of animals as a sacrificial atonement for sin. This priestly offering reached its culmination every year on the Day of Atonement. On this day, the Great High Priest entered the Holy of Holies and sprinkled the mercy seat of the Ark of the Covenant with the blood of an unblemished lamb to purify the people of sin and its effects. Thus, priesthood was intimately linked to offering the sacrificial body and blood, particularly that of an unblemished lamb.

In the New Testament, John the Baptist sees Jesus and cries, "Here is the Lamb of God who takes away the sin of the world!" (Jn 1:29). This statement would have sent a seismic shock through its hearers. John declares Jesus of Nazareth the sacrificial lamb who will give up his life in atonement for sin.

The Great High Priest

The Letter to the Hebrews takes this sacrificial theme and develops it even further. Jesus is presented as the Great High Priest who offers not the blood of bulls and goats for the forgiveness of sins, but his own blood on the new mercy seat of the cross. Hebrews 10:5 makes this priestly act of Christ crystal clear when it places these words on Christ's lips: "Sacrifices and offerings you have not desired, but a body you have prepared for me." Jesus' total, complete, and *priestly* gift of self to us on the cross purifies us of sin and its effects. Jesus literally gave his body and blood on the cross for the sanctification of the world. On the cross, the masculine body reaches its destiny and shines forth in its greatest perfection.

Every Man's Call

Every man is called to this same mission—to imitate Jesus' priestly act upon the cross by offering his body and blood for the sanctification of the world. A man's discernment isn't whether or not he should be a priest, but *how* God is calling him to be a priest—as an ordained priest to the Church, or as a spiritual priest to his family—the domestic church, or as a single man to transform society and culture from within.

Spiritual priesthood, then, is the male counterpart to spiritual motherhood. While some men are called to the ordained priesthood, *every man, without exception, is called to spiritual priesthood because priesthood is knit into the very structure of a man's being*. He offers his body and blood so others can draw closer to God. His life is a sacrificial offering not for material comfort, status, or power, but to purify his family, wife, neighborhood, and workplace of sin and its effects.

This idea of spiritual priesthood for all males, however, needs to be carefully distinguished from the ordained priesthood and the priesthood of the baptized. The ordained priesthood confers a special gift of the Holy Spirit that permits the exercise of a sacred power, which comes only from Christ himself through his Church (see *Catechism of the Catholic Church*, no. 1538). This is why a man can't declare himself an ordained priest on his own initiative nor on his own power. The power and authority of ordained priesthood flows from Christ through the Church, and it empowers a man to stand *in persona Christi*, in the person of Christ.

The priesthood of the baptized, also known as the common priesthood, originates in each person's baptismal graces. "The priesthood of the baptized" expresses the truth that *all* are consecrated in Christ to participate in his redemptive mission (see *Catechism of the Catholic Church,* nos. 1546–1537). Through the unfolding of our baptismal graces, we are oriented toward a life of holiness that seeks to transform the world and the workplace into the Kingdom of God, into a redeemed creation where God is present and active.[8]

This universal call to holiness and the charge to be co-laborers with Christ in building his Kingdom is further specified in *spiritual* priesthood for men. Just as women have a feminine vocation to spiritual motherhood, so too men have a masculine vocation to spiritual priesthood, which is to lay down their body and blood to purify the world of sin and its effects. Priesthood, like motherhood, is knit into the very structure of the body. Jesus *had* to be male. It was his masculine nature to give his body and blood away, just as it is a woman's feminine nature to receive and nurture new life.

The Fatherhood Connection

Embracing and living this call to spiritual priesthood is painfully countercultural in a society that has lost the distinctiveness of the priesthood and its orientation toward sacrifice and sanctification. Similarly, two other realities aggressively attacked today are motherhood and fatherhood. Abortion, contraception, embryonic stem cell research, and homosexual acts deny motherhood and fatherhood.

Sadly, the Church isn't exempt from these struggles. The current battle to remove masculine references to God in Scripture and the liturgy is a direct attack on the Fatherhood of God.

This attack on fatherhood affects the ordained priesthood as well. We don't call a priest "Master" or "Teacher" but "Father." A priest is a spiritual father. Spiritual priesthood and spiritual fatherhood overlap.

Why? Because of the profound truth of the masculine body. In order to become a human father, a man has to give his body and blood, his semen, away. New human life will never be conceived if a man withholds his biological gift of self.

The same is true on the spiritual plane. New spiritual life would never have been conceived if Jesus, the Great High Priest, had withheld his gift of self, if he hadn't given his body and blood away. The life-giving love of fatherhood complements and enhances the purifying love of priesthood. A spiritual father is a source of strength, protection, and exhortation. In the presence of a spiritual father, we feel an inner security to take risks to explore the world and act on it. In a complementary manner, a spiritual priest is a source of holiness, grace, and purity. In the presence of a spiritual priest, we feel inspired to lay down our lives and to imitate God's self-sacrificial love no matter what the cost. The two go together.

A Domestic Mission

If I were on a deserted island and could only have one chapter of Scripture, I'd pick Ephesians 5. This chapter not only talks about the great mystery of Christ's spousal love for the Church, but it also describes the priestly role of the husband:

> Husbands, love your wives, just as Christ loved the church
> and gave himself up for her, in order to make her holy by

cleansing her with the washing of water by the word, so as to present the church to himself in splendor, without a spot or wrinkle or anything of the kind—yes, so that she may be holy and without blemish. In the same way, husbands should love their wives as they do their own bodies. He who loves his wife loves himself. (Eph 5:25–28)

Christ is head of the Church in order to give his body up for her. A man is "head" of his wife not to stroke his own ego, but in order to give his body up for her.[9] I love the way Paul fills this passage in Ephesians 5 with priestly vocabulary: holy, purifying, immaculate, without stain or wrinkle, gave himself up, body, love.

When men drag their body and blood out of bed in the morning to pray and then lead their family in prayer, they're being priestly. When a man's body and blood go to work for the twenty-second year in a row, he's being priestly. When his body and blood resist the temptation to look at pornography or be unfaithful to his wife (even if she's his *future* wife), he's being priestly.

Priesthood, even spiritual priesthood, is incarnational. It happens in the body, not in some ultraspiritual realm. Priesthood requires the offering of flesh and blood.

Keepers of the Eucharist

In addition to sacrifice and spiritual fatherhood, priesthood has a third dimension. This is captured in the title of William Schaefers' classic book, *Keepers of the Eucharist.*[10]

As priests, men are keepers of the Eucharist. They are entrusted with the body and blood of Christ. This entrustment is obvious for the ordained priest, but what about men who are spiritual priests?

This is where our earlier reflections on Genesis can help us. All men, whether single or married, are entrusted with woman, with her body and blood. She is their eucharist, so to speak. They help make the eucharistic miracle happen in her life.

Divine Transformation

What is the eucharistic miracle? The ordinary elements of bread and wine become the body and blood of Christ. This same miracle is meant to happen in each of us. God wants to take the ordinary elements of our body and blood and transform them into the mystical body and blood of Christ.

Men help this happen in women. By receiving a woman's gift of self, affirming it and not trying to change it, a man awakens and heals in her the divine image. He helps heal the spousal meaning of the woman's body so she can make a sincere gift of self in all her feminine distinctiveness and potential for motherhood. Men help women fulfill their vocation to become the mystical body and blood of Christ in the world. John Paul II was very clear about this: "The acceptance of the woman by the man and the very way of accepting her, become, as it were, a first gift in such a way that the woman, in giving herself ... 'discovers herself' ... thanks to *the way* in which she has been received by the man."[11]

As keepers of the Eucharist and imitators of Christ, men have the special privilege of regarding women with the same reverence and tenderness as the Eucharist. When a man holds a woman, he holds the body of Christ in his hands.

A man's affirmation of woman as a feminine mirror of the divine image is so important. Hidden within the feminine personality is the Trinity: Daughter of the Father, mother of the Savior, and bride of the Spirit. When men affirm women in all their feminine distinctiveness and potential for motherhood, the female personality soars.

Ask any woman how she feels when men give her attention and affirmation without seeking anything in return. First, she's flabbergasted. Second, she soars. She feels free and energized to stretch, take risks, and fully develop her gifts and talents.

According to John Paul II, Christ acts in the same way as Bridegroom of the Church—he brings the Church to the fullness of her splendor, without spot or wrinkle.[12]

Seeds of Life

And that brings us to our final image, that of bridegroom. As spiritual priests, men are the bridegroom of the Church. They implant within the Church and the world the word of life.

A man's word and his presence are potent. He has the power to give life or take it away, to make God present in his family and workplace or deny God's existence. Every man is either a fertile contributor to the culture of life or a sterile pawn in the culture of death.

The Hebrew word for "male" is *zakar*, and it means "the remembering one."[13] Men are called to pass on the living memory of God in the world. They are not called to remain silent and allow Satan to spin his web of relational chaos and division, but to be like the New Adam, Jesus Christ, and speak forth the truth of man and woman's relationship with each other and God.

As the "remembering one," men preach Christ's total gift of self on the cross with their lives and words. They "make present" this gift of self at home, in the workplace, on the soccer field, and in the locker room. Fathers, uncles, youth ministers, teachers, and confessors must remind young men what our culture has forgotten: that men are made for union and communion through a sincere and fruitful gift of self.

By his word and witness, a man proclaims to the world that God is not a harsh, distant, and punitive father, but a loving, merciful, intimate, and forgiving father. John Paul II tirelessly incarnated this "remembering" presence in the world. He was a living icon of God's unconditional Fatherhood and Jesus' total emptying of self. The world will not forget the spiritual priesthood and fatherhood of Pope John Paul II!

Here Comes the Bride!

Finally, as male, spiritual priest, keeper of the Eucharist, and disseminator of the word, every man must be in living contact with God. By meditating on Jesus' relationship with the Father and gazing on the cross of Christ, men reencounter the origin and source of their masculine identity. In particular, each man must receive the spousal love of God and experience himself as the bride of Christ.

Yes, you read it right: I said "bride of Christ." This last area is often so off-putting for men! It's fairly easy for men to relate to God as Lord, Brother, Friend, Master, Shepherd, and Savior, but as Bride? You've got to be kidding. That's women's stuff.

No it isn't, and here's why (in the words of John Paul II): "In the Church every human being—male and female—is the 'Bride,' in that he or she accepts the gift of the love of Christ the Redeemer, and seeks to respond to it with the gift of his or her own person."[14]

In fact, throughout Scripture God images his relationship with his people as a husband to his bride (see Is 62:5, Hosea, and Rev 21:2–9). Jesus refers to himself as the Bridegroom in Matthew 9:15, Matthew 25:1–10, and John 3:29. Through this bridal imagery, the truth of God's relationship with his people as one of divine total self-giving is captured, a total self-giving that transmits God's very life.

Receiving the Bridegroom

Thus, to be bride means to receive the sincere gift of self of the bridegroom. Jesus Christ has given his body and blood to us as the Bridegroom. And so each of us is called to personally receive that gift as bride.

To really experience the depths of God's love, men only have to do one thing: become bride. They need to open themselves completely to Jesus' total gift of self and allow the Trinity to penetrate their being, not just their doing.

Whenever I broach this subject with men about being "bride," I see a simultaneous look of shock and determined resistance flash across their faces as they sound the trumpet of emotional retreat in their minds. This reaction is understandable if we're thinking in the category of male-to-male intimacy. However, John Paul II is offering a different category — that of bridal receptivity to God. To be "bride" means to stand before God in a posture of absolute receptivity to his love. For men who are willing to venture into this feminine-sounding territory, I'd like to offer some encouraging words for cultivating a spousal relationship with God that fits a more masculine mode of being:

1) Our model for spousal love is grounded in the Trinitarian relations, Father, Son, and Holy Spirit living in total union, total self-giving, total receiving, and total distinction. In this sense, the term "spousal love" is not being used in a sexual way but rather to describe the quality of total union and total self-giving and receiving that exists in God. In fact, Jesus' relationship to the Father has traditionally been described as one of total receptivity, as a "bridal" posture. I would encourage men to start by reflecting on the total self-giving and self-receiving love that is the Trinity and by asking for the grace to live in total self-giving, self-receiving union with God in imitation of the Trinitarian relations.

2) Our model for bridal love is based on Christ's love for the Church. Therefore, it may be helpful for men to initially image themselves in a spousal relationship with God not as an individual, but as part of the Church. In other words, they can imagine Christ's bridal love for the Church, of which they are a member. This "corporate identity" can feel a bit safer and less intimidating for men as it allows them to receive the love of the Bridegroom as a member of the "People of God."

3) Spousal love involves a shift in identity from an "I" to a "we," so a third approach is for men to begin to cultivate this same shift in their own identity. What do I mean? In a previous chapter I mentioned that one of the hallmarks of

a spousal relationship is that spouses carry a sense of their beloved with them wherever they go. Likewise, men can pray to shift their identity from accomplishing everything on their own to "I can do all things through Christ who strengthens me" (see Phil 4:13). In other words, every daily activity is approached as a "we," as a team effort between the man and Christ. It's rather like the difference between ice hockey and springboard diving. Ice hockey demands that each player shift his individual identity to a "we" effort in order to survive and thrive in the game. Diving, on the other hand, only requires one's own individual effort. A spousal life with God is like that team effort that flows from the "we" identity and leads to a thriving spiritual life.

4) Saint John of the Cross experienced a spousal relationship with God without losing one ounce of his masculinity. In fact, his bridal relationship with God inspired some of the most intimate spiritual poetry in the Catholic Church. What was his secret? Saint John related to God spousally through the feminine quality of his soul. In other words, he imaged his soul as feminine since in relationship to God the soul is always receptive. In this way, Saint John nourished his bridal relationship with God without any fear of losing his masculine identity. He learned to accept the gift of the love of Christ his Bridegroom and sought to respond to God with his own spousal gift. Men can take their cue from Saint John of the Cross and experience the receptive quality of their soul in relationship with God and seek to expand this bridal receptivity.

5) Mary is a fifth key for every man in fostering a spousal relationship with God. By taking Mary as his "lady" and open-

ing himself to a mystical, spousal union with her, a man's heart begins to absorb and experience spousal love of a different order—the supernatural order. This supernatural, spousal love with Mary creates a different mode of being within men that they can transfer to their relationship with God. When this happens, Mary fulfills her mission to lead every person, and indeed every man, to an intimate, spousal relationship with Christ.

Set Free

Through this process of opening himself more fully to God, a man discovers new things occurring. He's set free from fear of failure and the nagging dread of growing old alone. He no longer competes for power or pride of place, but seeks ways to serve and encourage others. He experiences release from addiction and the realignment of sexual desires and drives. His body is no longer simply a tool to get what he wants, but it becomes the very instrument of salvation for others.

A priestly man is a holy man. He stands behind the altar of his life and says to his wife, family, friends, and the world, "This is my body given up for you." Through this self-giving, men incarnate Christ the Bridegroom in the world.

Divine Model

I'm sure by now you've noticed that God's ways aren't our ways. For men to truly fulfill their masculine mission as spiritual priests, their spiritual journey must pass through bridal receptivity. While the masculine body indeed images the bridegroom aspect of God, men first need to fill themselves with the seminal life of God. Men need to personally experience the healing, intimate, and empowering love of God. Then they will understand from the inside out why Christ's divine love as Bridegroom is the model and pattern of all human love and men's love in particular.[15]

What a wonderful gift it is to be male and female, bride and bridegroom! As men imitate their Divine Bridegroom by offering their body and blood for the sanctification of the world, laboring right beside them are the Christian women God has called to be spiritual mothers by nurturing the emotional, moral, cultural, and spiritual life of others.

Spiritual motherhood and spiritual priesthood go hand in hand: as men lay down their bodies and blood to purify and redeem the world, so women lay down their lives for union. The result is astonishing. The more we are purified, the more we can live in union with each other and God. And the more we live in union with each other and God, the more we want to be purified so as to deepen that union.

A gender-neutral society is a sad and confused society. Discrimination is an evil, but distinction is God's design. Distinction creates beauty, uniqueness, unrepeatability, and passion for our specific contribution. The distinctions in the Trinity among Father, Son, and Holy Spirit imply no inequality but allow for uniqueness of relationship and mission.

The same is true on earth. The distinctions between male and female, spiritual priesthood and spiritual motherhood, bride and bridegroom all complement and explain one another. They give us our unique relationship and mission.

Let us beg the Holy Spirit to stir up this vision of spiritual priesthood in all men. Let us ask the Lord to bless and purify men everywhere so they can live a priestly life by offering their body and blood for the sanctification of the world.

QUESTIONS FOR REFLECTION AND DISCUSSION

1. Before reading this chapter, how would you have described the nature of the male?

2. In your relationships have you experienced passivity or domination resulting from original sin?

3. What is your reaction to the concept that spiritual priesthood is knit into the structure of a man's being?

4. If you are a man, how can you offer your body and blood for the sanctification of the world? If you're a woman, how can you help men develop their priestly charism?

5. What are your thoughts on men being "keepers of the Eucharist"?

6. What was your reaction to reading men have to first become bride?

7. Do you think that men and women having different responsibilities and roles is part of God's design or something that human society invented? Explain your answer.

8. Discuss how spiritual priesthood and spiritual motherhood go hand in hand.

FOR MEN

Consider the following ten suggestions for stirring up your priestly identity:

1. Read the Letter to the Hebrews.

2. Try to make one priestly (sacrificial) act a day.

3. Meditate on the Eucharist as a sacrifice sacrament, a communion sacrament, and a presence sacrament.

4. If you're married, pick one hour a week to watch the kids so your wife can spend the time in prayer or recreation.

5. Make a conscious effort to join yourself to the offering of the Eucharist at Mass.

6. Ask God every day: "What does it mean to be priest to my wife, family, friends, and co-workers?"

7. Read an account of Jesus' passion and death and consider: What happened when Jesus died?

8. Read *The Silence of Adam* by Larry Crabb.

9. Read *The Impact of God* by Iain Matthew (London: Hodder & Stoughton, 1995).

10. Read John Paul II's *On the Dignity and Vocation of Women* and meditate on the ways that women teach us about love and self-gift.

ᔰ CHAPTER 8 ᔰ

Women Priests: Why Not?

I THOUGHT THIS BOOK was complete until my mom read the manuscript. (Thanks, Mom!) Her one lingering question was, "What about women priests?" Being a good mother, she noticed that I had avoided one of the thorniest issues of our time. The question of women priests deserves an answer filled with integrity. It isn't an easy or simple answer. In fact, there isn't just one answer, but there are three: the head answer, the heart answer, and the faith answer.

The Head Answer

The head answer looks at Jesus' words and actions in the Bible to try to understand his intentions.[1]

First and foremost, the Bible says Christ chose twelve men as his apostles. While this fact is indisputable, the question remains, "Why?" Why did Jesus choose only men? Was it because of the cultural customs of his time? Was he restricted to men because women priests would have paralyzed the infant Church before it even started to walk?

Not a Conformist

If we look at Jesus' other actions in the Gospels, we clearly see he wasn't a conformist. Calling the Pharisees and Sadducees a "brood of vipers" and turning over the money changers' tables weren't exactly in line with Jewish customs. Jesus' interactions with women show a deliberate pattern of breaking Jewish and cultural norms. Here are a few examples:[2]

→ Jesus talked publicly with a Samaritan woman.

→ He took no notice of the legal impurity that resulted from being touched by the woman with a hemorrhage.

→ He allowed a woman sinner to wash his feet at the house of Simon the leper.

→ He pardoned with compassion the woman caught in adultery and showed that women shouldn't be judged more harshly than men.

→ He allowed women to accompany him in his ministry.

→ Women were the first witnesses of the resurrection and were charged with bringing that message to the apostles.

John Paul II described Christ's radical break with custom when he said: *"... in the eyes of his contemporaries, Christ became a promoter of women's true dignity* and of the *vocation* corresponding to this dignity. At times this caused wonder, surprise, often to the point of scandal ... because this behavior differed from that of his contemporaries."[3]

Most Qualified

Equally important is Mary's presence among Jesus' followers but not as one of the Twelve. If anyone qualified for ordained ministry, Mary did: she was sinless, docile to the Holy Spirit, and an intimate participant in God's plan of salvation. She had the inside track. She knew Jesus' mind and mission better than anyone else.

Yet, as Pope Innocent III noted in the thirteenth century, "Although the Blessed Virgin surpassed in dignity and excellence all the Apostles, nevertheless, it was not to her but to them that the Lord entrusted the keys of the kingdom."[4] We can't gloss over this decision. We can't simply attribute it to cultural pressures. In fact, Jesus chose the Twelve according to the Father's plan after spending the night in prayer.

New Circumstances

After Jesus' ascension, the apostles brought the Gospel into new situations and cultural circumstances. In Acts 1, Matthias was chosen to replace Judas Iscariot. Once again, Mary or any of the other women who had accompanied Jesus from the beginning of his ministry could have been considered, but weren't.[5]

Additionally, when Paul and others preached the Gospel and established churches among the Greeks, the ordained ministers were likewise male. In this Greek milieu, women priestesses were common. Women's ordination would have been readily accepted.[6] This would have been the ideal time to extend Jesus' nonprejudicial view of women to include priestly ministry, but it wasn't. Why?

The Heart Answer

The head can only take us only so far in understanding Jesus' actions. It must be complemented by the heart answer.

The heart answer looks beyond the data to penetrate the meaning or purpose of an action.

Beyond the Data

Let's take a quick example, a kiss. The head answer describes the data: two people meet, embrace, and one touches his lips to the other's cheek. But the heart answer asks: What is the meaning of this action or sign? Is it an expression of greeting, love, or betrayal? The heart answer tries to penetrate the visible expression of an action in order to grasp its invisible meaning.

In the Catholic Church, this dynamic of visible/invisible is encountered regularly in the sacraments. A sacrament expresses in a sensible manner something that is invisible and intangible.

The Matter Matters!

Priesthood is a sacrament. The priest represents Christ (the invisible reality) who acts through him (the visible reality). As early as the third century, Saint Cyprian made this quite clear: "The priest truly acts in the place of Christ."[7]

A sacrament by its very nature has to be expressed through matter. *And it matters what the matter is!*

Water, not chocolate milk, is used for baptism because water conveys washing, cleansing, purifying—the washing away of sin. Bread and wine are chosen for the Eucharist because they convey nourishment and the many becoming one. Potato chips are not good matter for this sacrament because the one becomes many. Likewise, a man is chosen for priesthood because he is able to stand *in persona Christi*, in the person of Christ.

A Female Hamlet?

Does it really matter if a man portrays Christ? Can't a woman portray him as well? This would be similar to asking if it really matters if a man portrays Hamlet. Wouldn't it be the same if a woman acted the part?

Obviously not. Hamlet is a man. He acts, thinks, fights, and loves like a man. We can't substitute a woman for the role and pretend everything is the same.

The same is true of priesthood. We can't substitute a woman for the male Christ and act as if everything is the same. In fact, the difference is even more significant. While an actor merely plays a role, the priest is sacramentally taking the place of Christ and acting in his name. In the Church's formal language, we say that the priest acts *in persona Christi*, in the person of Christ, not merely playing the role of Christ. When we see the priest at the altar with the eyes of faith, we see not just the man who is there but also Christ himself acting through the priest, offering his Eucharistic sacrifice to the Father.

Spousal Vision

A second heart reason why the priest must be a man is found in the spousal vision of the Church: the priest represents Christ the bridegroom, who is espoused to his bride the Church. The priest is not primarily an administrator, pastor, or preacher, but the bridegroom who offers his body and blood for his bride the Church.[8]

Unfortunately, we've lost this sense of spousal imagery between Christ and the Church. If a woman offers the body and blood of Christ at the altar, the spousal imagery is completely obscured. Bride is offering herself to bride. The bridegroom is eliminated. New spiritual life cannot be conceived.

In this view of priesthood, the distinction between men and women is irrelevant. A person of either gender is sufficient. We have become a Church of individuals rather than men and women who are bride and bridegroom.

Divine Distinction

This leads to the third and last heart reason—the divine distinction between men and women. The dignity, vocation, and mission of men and women are not based on social roles but are woven into the very structure of the body. Every woman is called to spiritual motherhood because her body visibly expresses the maternal gift of self. Every man is called to spiritual priesthood because his body visibly expresses the priestly gift of self.

Only men can be priests because priesthood is knit into a man's nature, to give his body and blood away. Only women can be mothers because motherhood is knit into a woman's nature, to receive and nurture new life. One does not detract from the other. They bring to the other the freedom to be what God has uniquely created them to be.

Power Play?

At this point, perhaps some readers still vehemently insist on priesthood for women as the only way to equality and power-sharing. I admit priesthood hasn't always been exercised as total self-giving service. In the past, women's participation in pastoral and administrative responsibilities within the Church has been restricted and even denied.

However, as we saw in chapter 3, John Paul II sought to change that. He asked the whole Church to foster feminine participation in its internal life in every way except for those sacramental tasks properly belonging to the priest. *Priesthood is not the last bastion of male superiority any more than motherhood is the last bastion of feminine superiority.*[9]

In this and the previous chapter, I've tried to show how priesthood is not about power but self-gift. Christ freely instituted a male priesthood not because of Jewish customs or cultural pressures, but because this choice represented a deeper reality—the male standing *in persona Christi* as bridegroom of the Church and an expression of the male's priestly nature.

This is the heart answer. However, there's still one more.

The Faith Answer

Ultimately, the male priesthood is a matter of faith. Christ revealed it that way, and we embrace it as an expression of divine revelation, not human logic. Other tenets of the faith fall into this mind-boggling category — the Trinity, the Incarnation, and the Real Presence in the Eucharist among others.

Beyond Logic

Human logic alone could never have deduced God as Three Persons in one. Who would have scripted the transcendent God being born in a stable with a fully human and divine nature? Who would have the gall to insist bread and wine could become the Body and Blood of God?

These are revealed doctrines of our faith that have been argued, maligned, denied, and misconstrued, just as many other doctrines have been throughout the centuries. For example, the Modalists wanted to preserve the oneness of God, so they dismissed Trinitarian communion. Arius denied the divinity of Christ and almost split the Church. The early Christians were accused of cannibalism, while many Protestant churches regard the bread and wine as only symbols.

If we add the male priesthood to this list of doctrines that have been attacked, I would say it's in very good company! Only when a cherished belief is threatened do we jump into the midst of it and try to understand it from God's point of view. This is precisely the case with male priesthood. The Church's constant tradition holds that the Church may not ordain women because she does not have the power *to change what Christ instituted*. Christ instituted a male priesthood, and this expressed intention was followed faithfully by his Apostles. Additionally, the matter of a sacrament can't be changed. Bread and wine will always be used for celebrating the Eucharist; a man and a woman will always be the "matter" for marriage; and a man will always stand *in persona Christi* for sacramental priesthood. The Church is fulfilling her responsibility to guard the deposit of faith, to guard what has been entrusted to her, because it reflects a deeper reality.

Pushing Theology Forward

The questioning of the male priesthood, just like the struggle with the Trinity, the Incarnation, and the Real Presence, can be fruitful. It can yield a fuller understanding of who God is in his nature and who we are in his image and likeness. It can illuminate anew the beauty and meaning of the sacraments that use ordinary, physical signs and symbols to make present invisible realities. It can also give us new language to speak about the mysteries of God while knowing full well that much remains veiled.

My prayer is that the head, heart, and faith of each Catholic would come to trust the teaching authority of the Church while seeking an ever deeper knowledge and understanding of the mysteries of the faith. The fruit of this trust will be vitally alive and authentically free women and men who make a passionate gift of their feminine and masculine selves to the world for the salvation of all.

QUESTIONS FOR REFLECTION AND DISCUSSION

1. Before reading this chapter, what were your thoughts about women priests? Has your perspective changed?

2. Have you ever thought of Jesus as breaking the cultural norms of his time when relating to women?

3. Do you think it matters what the "matter" is in priesthood? Why or why not?

4. How does a woman offering the sacrifice of the Mass affect the spousal imagery between Christ and the Church?

5. What areas in Church life would you like to see women more involved in? How can you help that happen?

☙ CHAPTER 9 ❧

Women in the Third Millennium

"WHERE THERE IS no vision, the people perish" (see Prov 29:18).[1] Today we might say, "Without a mission, women get depressed."

Emotional Roadkill

When women have no sense of mission, no sense of their journey's purpose, they're emotional roadkill—easily flattened on the pavement of life. The real tragedy for many women is feeling suction-cupped to an insignificant life. What they do is an unnoticeable blip on the global screen of life. How do we peel ourselves off this depressive pavement?

A change in perspective always helps, especially when it's drawn from the wisdom of the Church. Can you guess where the following statement is from?

As you know, the Church is proud to have glorified and liberated woman ... to have brought into relief her basic equality with man. But the hour is coming, in fact has come, when the vocation of woman is being achieved in its fullness, the hour in which woman acquires in the world an influence, an effect, and a power never hitherto achieved. That is why, at this moment when the human race is undergoing so deep a transformation, women impregnated with the spirit of the Gospel can do so much to aid mankind in not falling.[2]

This is an excerpt from the Second Vatican Council's closing statement to women. Written in 1965, it rings true today. Women have achieved an influence that surpasses previous times and ages.

A Varied Past

Until the mid-nineteenth century, women in the United States couldn't go to college or inherit property. Only in the twentieth century were they allowed to vote and continue a professional career after marriage.

In the third millennium, women are CEOs, politicians, administrators, and business owners. They are doctors, lawyers, engineers, graphic artists, and teachers. Their presence is felt within the sphere of public life as well as the private sphere of the home. They are anything but insignificant.

At the same time, global society and culture are undergoing rapid changes that shake the foundations of human life. The memory of God is being rubbed out from schools, public places, and national constitutions. Economic systems are crumbling, and aggression and violence rip nations apart. For many women, advances in technology and medicine are elusive.

Open Wide the Doors to Christ!

But John Paul II, our witness to hope, never became discouraged. From the first moment of his pontificate, one theme trumpeted from his lips, "Be not afraid!"

His first papal homily on October 22, 1978, began with these words:

> Do not be afraid! Open, indeed, open wide the doors to Christ! Open to his saving power the confines of states, and systems political and economic, as well as the vast fields of culture, civilization, and development. Do not be afraid![3]

To open every door of human life to the person of Christ is the mission of women in the third millennium. Because women have acquired "an influence, effect, and power hitherto unachieved," they can open wide the door to Christ in settings and circumstances previously shielded from the Gospel.

Guardians of the Future

The Council's statement also begged women to "watch carefully over the future of our race. Hold back the hand of man who, in a moment of folly, might attempt to destroy human civilization."[4] It reminded women that they are the first educators of their children, passing on to them the rich traditions of word and sacrament.

A woman's mission today is the same as that of the first disciples: be leaven in the world. Remake the fabric of culture and society into a Christian one. Transform the marketplace from within. Build a civilization of love. Be the Body of Christ on earth! Live your feminine genius!

Root, Shoot, and Fruit

This mission, however, must flow from a woman's dignity and vocation. Without being properly rooted, she will be like seed sown in rocky soil, springing up for a time, but withering under the burden and toil of day-to-day life.

Embedding the Root

We can never begin with mission; it is the fruit. Instead, we must begin with the root—our dignity as daughters. This dignity embeds us in the nourishing heart of the Father from which we draw our natural value and worth. In turn, we can experience God sending forth a shoot into the world, our feminine body. We must never forget that our vocation and mission in the world extend from our rootedness as daughters.

Sending Forth the Shoot

But the root is not the same as the shoot. The shoot extends forth and gives visible expression to what is hidden and unseen. The shoot of the feminine body encloses within it the special capacity for motherhood.

As the shoot matures, it sends forth the vines and leaves of spiritual motherhood, which entwine their presence into the moral, cultural, economic, political, and spiritual life of family and society. These bring into the public and private spheres a woman's capacity for self-giving, for seeing others with the heart, for valuing the dignity of each person, and for nurturing life.

Bearing the Fruit

The root and the shoot thus prepare the way for the fruit. They anchor and nourish a woman's dignity and identity so she is free to blossom. What is the fruit? It is her unique and unrepeatable presence in the world. It is a woman's passionate sense of having something to give at this time in history and her collaboration in the redemption of mankind. It is the fullness of the feminine genius impacting family, society, and culture.

In Full Blossom

A woman's being and personality fully blossom when she experiences within herself the cross and the incarnation, when she bears Christ to the world while participating in the sufferings of Christ.

Through this interior marriage of the incarnation and cross, she participates in the indwelling of the Trinity. She and the Father are united, and through their spousal life in the Holy Spirit, the fruits of faith, hope, and love mature in her in order to bear Christ to the world.

This, then, is a woman's unique and unrepeatable mission in the world. It is neither root nor shoot, but the fruit of her dignity as a daughter and her vocation as a woman. It is part of the organic whole God made her to be as her feminine identity and genius flower in the world.

More Than Our Functions

As women in the third millennium, we must keep this multifaceted vision before us. The pressures of work, mothering, cooking, and laundry constantly try to reduce us to our roles. They want to squeeze us into our functions and convince us that these are the mainstay of our worth and identity.

We must resist being reduced to our roles. We must resist being applauded for our doing while forgetting about our being. Women are more complicated than this. We are being and doing. We are unique individuals and mothers. We are interior and exterior. We are a coexistence of many opposites.

Our identity is a composite of our dignity, vocation, and mission. It is root, shoot, and fruit, all organically connected into one presence in the world.

Diamonds in the Light

This is the great vision of women the Catholic Church holds before us. It's the vision that should give us peace, hope, and joy as we navigate the twists and turns of life. It should peel us off the pavement and set us free to walk upright, drawing emotional strength and courage from the truth of God's word pulsating within us.

The Church rejoices in having glorified and liberated women in her midst. These women are diamonds in the Light, radiating the true dignity, vocation, and mission of women from the outback of Australia to the Kenai Peninsula of Alaska. This is every woman's journey marvelously manifested through the feminine genius revealing God's presence in the world.

QUESTIONS FOR REFLECTION AND DISCUSSION

1. What was your reaction to Vatican II's "Closing Message to Women"?

2. Do you feel glorified and liberated by the Church? Why or why not?

3. Does it help to image your dignity, vocation, and mission as a root, shoot, and fruit? Why or why not?

4. How can you make a difference in the Church and the world as a woman in the third millennium?

5. What are the most significant thoughts and ideas you've gained from this book?

6. How has your view of the "feminine genius" and "every woman's journey" changed by reading this book?

7. Write a prayer to the Holy Spirit asking for the grace to live your dignity, vocation, and mission as a woman in the third millennium.

Notes

CHAPTER 1

First a Daughter, Then a Bride

1. Mary Reed Newland, *How to Raise Good Catholic Children* (Manchester, NH: Sophia Institute Press, 2004. Original title: *We and Our Children*, 1954); *The Year and Our Children* (Manchester, NH: Sophia Institute Press, 2007).

CHAPTER 2

Why Male and Female?

1. For a detailed review of ancient and medieval thinking on women, see Prudence Allen, RSM, *The Concept of Woman: The Aristotelian Revolution, 750 BC–AD 1250* (Grand Rapids, MI: Wm. B. Eerdmans Publishing Co., 1997) and *The Concept of Woman: The Early Humanist Reformation, 1250–1500* (Grand Rapids, MI: Wm. B. Eerdmans Publishing Co., 2006).

2. John Paul II, *Man and Woman He Created Them: A Theology of the Body*, trans. Michael Waldstein (Boston: Pauline Books & Media, 2006).

3.Ibid., 157.

4. Ibid., 163.

5. *Many people wonder why I include both union and communion in this description.* Each word brings out a different nuance. Union often has a more physical connotation (the marital union of husband and wife), while

communion implies interpersonal relationship (the communion of the Trinity). As human persons, we are created with the capacity for both bodily union and relational communion.

6. John Paul II, *On the Dignity and Vocation of Women* (Boston: Pauline Books & Media, 1988), no. 7.

7. My description of the Trinity is not meant to indicate a time sequence, as if the Father and Son existed before the Spirit. The self-giving of Father and Son and the bursting forth of the Spirit are eternal.

8. See John Gray, *Men Are from Mars, Women Are from Venus* (New York: HarperCollins, 1992); *Mars and Venus in Love* (New York: HarperCollins, 1996); *Mars and Venus on a Date* (New York: HarperPerennial, 1997); *The Mars and Venus Diet and Exercise Solutions* (New York: St. Martin's Press, 2003).

Chapter 3

The Feminine Genius

1. John Paul II, *Man and Woman*, 181.

2. Ibid., 182.

3. John Paul II, *On the Dignity and Vocation of Women*, no. 18.

4. John Paul II, *Letter to Women* (Boston: Pauline Books & Media, 1995).

5. John Paul II, *The Gospel of Life* (Boston: Pauline Books & Media, 1995), no. 86.

6. See John Paul II, *On the Dignity and Vocation of Women*, nos. 17–22.

7. John Paul II, *The Genius of Women* (Washington, DC: United States Conference of Catholic Bishops, 1997), Angelus Reflection of July 23, 1995.

8. Ibid., World Day of Peace Message, January 1, 1995.

9. Ibid., Angelus Reflection of September 3, 1995.

10. Ibid.

11. John Paul II, *The Genius of Women*, Welcome to Gertrude Mongella, Secretary General of the Fourth World Council on Women, May 1995, no. 8.

12. Ibid., no. 3

13. See also John Paul II, *The Role of the Christian Family in the Modern World* (Boston: Pauline Books & Media, 1981), no. 23.

14. John Paul II, *Letter to Women*, no. 10.

CHAPTER 4

Sin and the Spousal Meaning of the Body

1. The *Catechism of the Catholic Church*, no. 376, describes our life of union (harmony) this way: "By the radiance of this grace [the grace of sharing in divine life] all dimensions of man's life were confirmed. As long as he remained in the divine intimacy, man would not have to suffer or die. The inner harmony of the person, the harmony between man and woman, and finally the harmony between the first couple and all creation, comprised the state called 'original justice.'"

2. John Paul II, *Man and Woman*, 237.

3. Quoted from the *New International Version* of the Bible.

4. John Paul II, *Man and Woman*, 251.

5. Ibid., 242.

6. Ibid., 243–244.

7. Ibid., 254.

8. John Paul II, *On the Dignity and Vocation of Women*, no. 10.

9. A wonderful book on the topic of feminine friendships is *The Friendships of Women* by Dee Brestin (Colorado Springs, CO: Cook Communications Ministries, 2009).

10. John Paul II, *Man and Woman*, 287–288.

11. See John Paul II, *Man and Woman*, 257.

CHAPTER 5

Weaving a Tapestry of Life

1. See *The Collected Works of Edith Stein, Volume 2*, "Essays on Woman," trans. Freda Mary Oben (Washington, DC: ICS Publications, 1987).

2. See John Paul II, *Man and Woman,* 391–392.

3. Marie-Dominique Philippe, OP, *The Morning Star* (Peoria, IL: Congregation of Saint John, 1989), 254.

4. John Paul II, *Man and Woman*, 420.

5. Saint Symeon the New Theologian as quoted in John Paul II, *Vita Consecrata* (Boston: Pauline Books & Media, 1996), no. 20.

6. Hans Urs von Balthasar, *You Crown the Year with Your Goodness: Sermons Throughout the Liturgical Year* (San Francisco: Ignatius Press, 1989), 24.

CHAPTER 6

The Spouse of the Spirit

1. Scott Hahn, *The Lamb's Supper* (New York: Doubleday, 1999).

2. Christopher West, *Good News About Sex & Marriage: Answers to Your Honest Questions about Catholic Teaching* (Ann Arbor, MI: Servant Publications, 2000), 21.

3. Saint Joseph Communications (www.saintjoe.com or 800-526-2151) is an excellent resource for tapes and CDs about the Catholic faith. Also, Our Father's Will Communications (www.theologyofthebody.net or 866-333-6392) carries Katrina Zeno's talks and retreats on tape and CD along with numerous resources on the theology of the body and other topics.

4. All these publications are available from Pauline Books & Media (www.pauline.org).

5. The thirteenth-century Franciscan theologian Blessed John Duns Scotus speaks of Mary's great need in his *Ordinatio* III, distinction 3, question 1.

6. See John Paul II, *On the Dignity and Vocation of Women*, no. 11.

CHAPTER 7

What About the Men?

1. John Paul II did, however, offer some invaluable reflections about human fatherhood in his apostolic exhortation on Saint Joseph entitled *Guardian of the Redeemer* (Boston: Pauline Books & Media, 1989).

2. John Paul II, *Man and Woman*, 197.

3. See John Paul II, *On the Dignity and Vocation of Women*, no.14.

4. See John Paul II, *Man and Woman*, 195.

5. See John Paul II, *Man and Woman*, 260, where, in speaking about lust, the pope says: "The relationship of the gift is changed into a relationship of appropriation."

6. Larry Crabb, *The Silence of Adam* (Grand Rapids, MI: Zondervan, 1998).

7. Lorene Hanley Duquin, *They Called Her the Baroness* (Staten Island, NY: Alba House, 1995).

8. Another way to summarize these distinctions in priesthood would be through the following schema:

— Christ for the Church;

   — The ordained priest in Christ's place in the Church;

      — Priesthood of all the baptized for the world at large;

         — The father in his family;

            — Each man for the people in his own life.

9. See John Paul II, *On the Dignity and Vocation of Women*, no. 24.

10. William Henry Schaefers, *Keepers of the Eucharist* (Milwaukee, WI: Bruce Publishing Co., 1946).

11. John Paul II, *Man and Woman*, 196.

12. See John Paul II, *On the Dignity and Vocation of Women*, no. 24.

13. Crabb, *The Silence of Adam*, 79.

14. John Paul II, *On the Dignity and Vocation of Women*, no. 25.

15. Ibid.

CHAPTER 8
Women Priests: Why Not?

1. For a detailed explanation of the Catholic Church's teaching on women and the ordained priesthood, see: Sacred Congregation for the Doctrine of the Faith, *On the Question of the Admission of Women to the Ministerial Priesthood (Inter Insigniores)* (Boston: Pauline Books & Media, 1976), and John Paul II, *On Reserving Priestly Ordination to Men Alone (Ordinatio Sacerdotalis)* (Boston: Pauline Books & Media, 1994). See also Sara Butler, *The Catholic Priesthood and Women: A Guide to the Teaching of the Church* (Mundelein, IL: Hillenbrand Books, 2007).

2. See *On the Question of the Admission of Women to the Ministerial Priesthood*, nos. 10–11.

3. John Paul II, *On the Dignity and Vocation of Women*, no. 12.

4. As quoted in *On the Question of the Admission of Women to the Ministerial Priesthood*, no. 11.

5. See ibid.

6. *On the Question of the Admission of Women to the Ministerial Priesthood*, no. 15.

7. As quoted in *On the Question of the Admission of Women to the Ministerial Priesthood*, no. 25.

8. John Paul II says, "The Eucharist ... is the Sacrament of the Bridegroom and of the Bride" (*On the Dignity and Vocation of Women*, no. 26).

9. The Catholic Church makes a distinction between the ordained priesthood and the baptismal priesthood. Every Christian by means of baptism is baptized into Christ's mission as priest, prophet, and king. Women share in this baptismal priesthood and therefore are called to offer their bodies as a living sacrifice (see Rom 12:1) just as men are called to be nurturing. However, because of divine revelation, which is also revealed through the structure of the body, the dominant charism in women is (spiritual and biological) motherhood and in men is (spiritual and ordained) priesthood.

CHAPTER 9
Women in the Third Millennium

1. Quoted from the *King James* version of the Bible.

2. *The Documents of Vatican II*, "Closing Message to Women," (Chicago: Follett Publishing Company, 1966), ed. Walter M. Abbott, SJ; trans. Joseph Gallagher.

3. John Paul II's first papal homily (October 22, 1978: AAS 79 [1978]), 947.

4. *The Documents of Vatican II*, "Closing Message to Women."

Katrina J. Zeno is co-founder of Women of the Third Millennium (www.wttm.org) and the founding coordinator of the John Paul II Resource Center for the Diocese of Phoenix, Arizona. A popular retreat speaker, she is the author of *The Body Reveals God: A Guided Study of Pope John Paul II's Theology of the Body* and *When Life Doesn't Go Your Way*.  Katrina is an avid hiker, Argentine tango enthusiast, and the blessed mother of a young-adult son, Michael.

BOOKS & MEDIA

The Daughters of St. Paul operate book and media centers at the following addresses. Visit, call or write the one nearest you today, or find us on the World Wide Web, www.pauline.org.

CALIFORNIA
3908 Sepulveda Blvd, Culver City, CA 90230	310-397-8676
2640 Broadway Street, Redwood City, CA 94063	650-369-4230
5945 Balboa Avenue, San Diego, CA 92111	858-565-9181

FLORIDA
145 S.W. 107th Avenue, Miami, FL 33174	305-559-6715

HAWAII
1143 Bishop Street, Honolulu, HI 96813	808-521-2731
Neighbor Islands call:	866-521-2731

ILLINOIS
172 North Michigan Avenue, Chicago, IL 60601	312-346-4228

LOUISIANA
4403 Veterans Memorial Blvd, Metairie, LA 70006	504-887-7631

MASSACHUSETTS
885 Providence Hwy, Dedham, MA 02026	781-326-5385

MISSOURI
9804 Watson Road, St. Louis, MO 63126	314-965-3512

NEW YORK
64 W. 38th Street, New York, NY 10018	212-754-1110

PENNSYLVANIA
9171-A Roosevelt Blvd, Philadelphia, PA 19114	215-676-9494

SOUTH CAROLINA
243 King Street, Charleston, SC 29401	843-577-0175

VIRGINIA
1025 King Street, Alexandria, VA 22314	703-549-3806

CANADA
3022 Dufferin Street, Toronto, ON M6B 3T5	416-781-9131

¡También somos su fuente para libros,
videos y música en español!